PSYCHO-SOCIAL CORRELATES OF ACHIEVEMENT

PSYCHO-SOCIAL CORRELATES OF ACHIEVEMENT

Ms. BALUSU VEENA KUMARI
Sir C.R.R. College of Education, Eluru-6
West Godavari Dist., A. P., India

Editor
DR. DIGUMARTI BHASKARA RAO
R. V. R. College of Education,
D–43, Srinivasa Nagar,
Guntur–522006 (A.P.)

DISCOVERY PUBLISHING HOUSE
NEW DELHI-110 002

Published by:

DISCOVERY PUBLISHING HOUSE PVT. LTD.
4383/4B, Ansari Road, Darya Ganj
New Delhi-110 002 (India)
Phone : +91-11-23279245; 23253475; 43596065
E-mail : discoverybooksindia@gmail.com
discoverypublishinghouse@gmail.com
namitwasan9@gmail.com
web : www.discoverypublishinggroup.com

***First Published:* 2003**
***Reprinted:* 2022**

ISBN: 978-81-7141-547-2

Psycho-social Correlates of Achievement

Printed at:
Infinity Imaging Systems
Delhi

PREFACE

Education has become indispensable for every one. The effectiveness of any educational system is gauged to the extent the students involved in the system achieve, whether it be in cognitive conative or psycho-motor domain, as the academic achievement is of paramount importance in the present socio-economic and cultural contexts. Educational planners, heads of institutions, curriculum designers, researchers, teachers and others who are involved in the task of helping students to achieve better would like to have a knowledge of the extent of the influence the achievement correlates exert on achievement.

This study, in this direction, has been taken up to identify the influence of socio-economic status and educational aspirations on academic achievement. This study has identified no relationship between socio-economic status and achievement in social studies and a positive relationship between educational aspirations and achievement in social studies. These results are one way opposing and the other way supporting the earlier research findings. A close study of the results of this study will help a lot in enhancing the socio-economic status, educational aspirations and academic achievement of secondary school students.

Dr. Veena Kumari
Dr. Bhaskara Rao

CONTENTS

1

INTRODUCTION

INTRODUCTION

An individual, with an all-round development, becomes a responsible, dynamic, resourceful and enterprising citizen with a strong good moral character and uses all his capacities to develop his own self, his society and his nation to the highest extent by contributing his best to the national honour, national glory, national culture and civilization.

Education, on one hand, develops full personality of an individual by making him intelligent, learned, bold, courageous, strong and good at character a part from its contribution to the growth and development of society in particular and nation in general. Education is alone the medium of making transfer from one generation to another, the spiritual values, moral ideals, aspirations of the nation, and its cultural heritage in order that they can be preserved, purified and utilized to sublimate ideas of the people into higher achievements. Not only an individual but also the society is immensely benefited with the choice attainments through education.

The process of education is quite social as a child is exposed to learning in a congenial climate. The elders of the society pass on their own experiences, interests, purposes and dispositions to the less matured members of the society. The children would learn the mode of behaviour, formulate attitudes, and pick-up essential skills by seeming the elders, by mixing with them and by talking with them and hearing them. It is a process of cordial rapport between a master and his disciple.

In modern days the concept of 'education as a social function' has not changed, but the methods have changed. In the primitive days the society was not as complex as it is today and therefore it was then very simple for the society to transmit its experiences to the new generations. But, today's society being complex in its knowledge and skills, it cannot itself transmit all these directly to the fast rising new generation. Now there is a need for an organized formal institution to impart the essential knowledge and fundamental skills. Hence, the need for a school. But, the establishment of a school does not preclude the role of other social agencies like home, church, radio, press, T.V. and several other influences of the environment. The school is only a selected and controlled environment.

The concept of formal education has a wider meaning and includes an educational set-up. At present, on the Indian educational scene, we follow the 10+2+3 pattern suggested by the Education Commission (1964-66). In these three stages, 10th Class is a crucial one in many aspects as it possesses adolescents and forms the basis for selecting various disciplines and acts as a stage between childhood and adulthood.

STATEMENT OF THE PROBLEM

To identify the important role of Socio-Economic Status and Educational Aspirations in deciding the level of Achievement in Social Studies, the present study is entitled *"A Study of Socio-Economic Status and Educational Aspirations of Secondary School Students in relation to their Achievement in Social Studies."*

NEED FOR THE STUDY

Life in general and for a student in particular has become highly competitive. Today there is no place for a mediocre student, there is a limited room at the top, that too only for the best. Almost all the attractive courses and positions have competitive tests. A student with an ambition to secure admission into such courses and positions should have a dedicated and methodical approach towards these tests. The basic subject material for these tests is available from the secondary level classes. Secondary school education prepares the ground necessary for the students to join different disciplines which qualify them for competitive courses or jobs.

A student, with good socio-economic status joins such school as imparts desirable quality education and he or she benefits with enough competence for higher educational qualifications. One can also say that a student even without reasonable socio-economic status will also score well in the examinations and possesses high educational aspirations. Studies show that there is no relationship among the factors like socio-economic status, educational aspirations and achievements. These results vary from sample to sample, place to place, time to time and educational level to educational level.

Based on the research results available an indepth study is required at various educational levels, sample study of tenth class with regard to their socio-economic status, educational aspirations and achievement in social studies and the relationship between socio-economic status and achievement in social studies, and educational aspirations and achievement in social studies.

OBJECTIVES OF THE STUDY

Everyone works with set objectives in order to get benefits by achieving those objectives. Likewise for this study, *"A Study of Socio-Economic Status and Educational Aspirations of Secondary School Students in relation to their Achievement in Social Studies"*, the following objectives are framed for the present study:

1. To find out the socio-economic status of secondary school students.
2. To find out the educational aspirations of secondary school students.
3. To find out the achievement in social studies of secondary school students.
4. To find out the relationship between socio-economic status and achievement in social studies of secondary school students.
5. To find out the relationship between educational aspirations and achievement in social studies of secondary school students.
6. To identify the difference in the level of socio-economic status, educational aspirations, achievement in social studies, relationship between socio-economic status and achievement in social studies

and relationship between educational aspirations and achievement in social studies in secondary school students of residential and non-residential schools, private and government schools, rural and urban schools, Telugu medium and English medium schools and in boys and girls.

SCOPE OF THE STUDY

One of the most important outcomes of any educational set-up is the achievement of the students. Depending on the level of the achievement, individuals are characterised as high achievers, average achievers and low achievers. Many studies at different stages of education indicate that the academic achievement is dependant on variables like school set-up and its organisation, socio-economic status of students, and their educational aspirations. Besides this, the personal characteristics, vocational aspirations, creativity, intelligence, adjustment, attitudes, values, etc., will play their legitimate role. But socio-economic status and educational aspirations play a major role. But socio-economic status and educational aspirations play a major role. Hence, this study is confined only to socio-economic status and educational aspirations in relation to achievement in social studies.

IMPORTANCE OF THE STUDY

The effectiveness of any educational system is gauged to the extent the students-involved in the system-achieve, whether it be in cognitive, conative or psychomotor domain. In general terms achievement refers to the scholastic or academic achievement of the student at the end of an educational programme. To maximize the achievement within a given set-up is, therefore, the goal of every educationist. Research has come to our aid by looking into what variables—personal, home, college, teacher etc., promote achievement and what are deterrents to it. It has been thus indicated that a good number of variables, such as personality characteristics of the learners, the socio-economic status from which they hail, the educational aspirations, the organizational climate of the school, etc., to mention a few, influence achievement in varying degrees.

Heads of institutions, curriculum planners, teachers and others who are involved in the task of helping students to achieve better would like to have knowledge of the extent of influence these correlates exert on achievement. Further, a synoptic view of the researches done would be of utmost importance to the educational researcher to enable him to explore greater depths in this rather important area of achievement.

Behind these arguments, there is an assumption that the students will benefit from the academic excellence provided their teachers look into the merits and demerits of what and how they are learning and take necessary steps to enhance their academic achievement.

This study identifies the achievement in social studies of secondary school students. If the factors concerned with high achievement are identified, they will be extended to the average and low performers.

Recent years have witnessed increasing public concern with the plight of the socially disadvantaged. Psychologists, long back interested in the study of possible differences among individuals of varied social and economic backgrounds, have played a significant role by translating this concern into practical knowledge. Developmentalists have particular interest in trying to understand the relationship between development and factors behind the disadvantaged. Many studies are confined to the effects of socio-economic status.

Since the society in India, as elsewhere, consists of different classes, it is but natural for the researchers to think of the extent to which home-conditions influence the scholastic achievement of children. These home-conditions, which are generally known as the socio-economic status, may be further sub-divided as parent's occupation and education, family income, family possession, and social participation. Researchers generally include socio-economic status as one of the variables in their studies. The present study considers the relationship between socio-economic status and achievement. In this present study, after identifying the relationship between achievement and socio-economic status of the students, the researcher attempts to explore the factors that presumably are relevant to the upliftment of socio-economically disadvantaged.

Aspiration is a longing for what is above with advancement as its goal. It emphasizes the desire to improve or to rise above one's present status. An individual's aspiration level represents him not only as he is at a particular moment, but also what he would like to be at some point in the future. It is also a measure of his deliberate disposition, an important element of his long range behaviour.

The educational aspirations help a student to achieve them. For this he has to work hard, understand well, and apply perfectly. Previous studies indicate that there is a positive relationship between aspirations vocational and aspirations educational and achievement. Hence this study intends to know the level of educational aspirations of secondary school students and its association with the achievement in social studies.

Considering the importance of socio-economic status, educational aspirations and achievement in social studies, the present study examines the level of socio-economic status, educational aspirations and achievement in social studies, relationship between socio-economic status and educational aspirations, and relationship between educational aspirations and achievement in social studies at secondary school level.

EDUCATIONAL IMPLICATIONS

The major educational implications of the present study are:

1. Measures will be taken to improve the socio-economic status of the students and their families through various social welfare programmes in case of their low socio-economic status.
2. Measures will be taken to improve the level of educational aspirations, wherever they are found low with the students.
3. The factors involved in high achievement will be extended to other achievement groups and simultaneously the causes for middle or lower achievement, if exist, can be rectified.
4. The socio-economic status, one of the correlates of achievement, can be improved or at least its positive influence on achievement will be identified.
5. Educational aspirations, the future goals of life, may be suitably moulded depending on the level of students.

6. If there exists any positive relationship between socio-economic status and achievement in social studies, and educational aspirations and achievement in social studies, proper measures will be taken to promote such relationship.
7. The relationship, positive or negative, or achievement in social studies with socio-economic status and educational aspirations may help the educators and administrators to take up necessary decisions to help the students.

2

REVIEW OF RELATED LITERATURE

Research in a particular faculty requires adequate knowledge related to the subject and it is essential to know what has been done in the same area. A summary of writings of recognised authorities and previous research provides an evidence of what has already been known and what is still unknown and untested. An effective research activity, without giving any scope for duplication of work indicates useful hypotheses and helpful suggestions for significant investigation.

Citing studies that show substantial agreement and those that seem to present conflicting conclusions help to sharpen and define understanding of existing knowledge in the problem area, provide a background for the research project, and makes the investigator aware of the status of the issue. Parading a long list of annotated studies relating to the problem is ineffective and inappropriate. Only those studies that are plainly relevant, competently executed, and clearly reported should be included.

Capitalizing on the reviews of expert researchers can be fruitful in providing helpful ideas and suggestions. While review articles that summarize related studies are useful, they do not provide a satisfactory substitute for an independent research. Even though the review of related literature is not a substitute for an independent work, it is one of the first steps in the research process. It is a valuable guide to define the problem, to recognize its significance, to suggest promising data-gathering devices, to appropriate the study design, and sources of data for effective analysis and to arrive at fruitful conclusions.

The search for related literature is a time consuming process, even though it is necessary, as earlier stated, for a good research work. Hence this chapter, Review of Related Literature, is meant for the study of achievement correlates namely, socio-economic status and educational aspirations.

ACHIEVEMENT

Education plays a vital role in building a society. A modern society cannot achieve its aims of economic growth, technical development and cultural advancement without fully harnessing the talents of its citizens. Educationists thus strive to develop fully the intellectual potential of the students and make efforts to see that their potentialities are fully realized and channelized for the benefit of the individuals and that of the society.

Educational opportunities, though open to all, do not seem to engage to any reasonable extent the capacities of those who seek to utilize them. An eternal question baffling parents, educators and national planners is: "Why do students of demonstrated ability flop in their academic efforts at school or college examinations?" Academic under-achievement, more than academic failure, constitutes a grave problem as it amounts to wastage of human resources which is construed as an irreparable loss to the society, which a developing country like ours can ill afford. This stimulated a number of researchers to undertake studies, like the present study, on factors influencing achievement a review of which is presented here under.

The concept of over-achievement and under-achievement, logically speaking, is meaningful in relation to some expected level of performance. Theoretically, if one's performance is superior to the expected standard, one may be regarded as over-achiever, whereas when one's performance is inferior, one may be regarded as under-achiever.

The scientists like Stanley, Ross, Frumar and Frazen feel that the over-achievement phenomenion is, logically, spurious and meaningless, since no one can operate above one's potentiality level, from which quite often the standard of one's expected performance is derived. However, they assert that under-achievement is indicative of one's ability. On accepting the verdict and the theoretical definition of the under-achievement concept which is proportionate to one's actual performance, we are justified to ask from which level the expected performance comes.

Broadly speaking, there are two ways open for answering the question regarding the standard of expected performance. Either, the standard of expected performance may be subjective, or it may be objective. The subjective standard of expected performance may further be classified into two categories. In one type of the subjective standard of expected performance, the individual himself determines the standard of performance; whereas in the second type of subjective standard, the expected standard of performance is stipulated by the person who is operating as a 'significant-other' (parent or teacher) in one's process of socialization. We all know that the subjective standard of performance determined by significant others is so much subjective and irrational that it is rarely attainable. How-so-ever hard a student may try, it is not possible to satisfy one's parents or teachers through his achievement.

Psychologically speaking, the subjective standard of expected performance, irrespective of the fact, whether it is arising from within or it is imposed by the parents or teachers from outside, represents man's hopes and aspirations which are endless.

One more type of the subjective standard of expected performance represents aspirations and hopes of one's spiritual leader or hero. Such a standard of expected performance is most often unrealizable and may be termed as the ideal standard of expected performance.

The expected standard of performance which comes from within the individual, is the outcome of his own aspirations and satisfactions related to his achievements. Previous experiences of success result in guiding a person for raising his level of expectation. Some individuals may be satisfied with the previous achievement while others may want to struggle for higher grades. They are often eager to learn more, confident of doing it and ambitious of achieving more.

Taylor states that the value the student places upon his own worth effects his academic achievement. Very low level of expectation tends to make a pupil accept very low standard of achievement, very high expectations lead to discouragement and diminished effort because he feels he cannot live upto what is required of him. To be practical, the level of expectation needs to be geared to suit each individual capability.

Many changes are being, witnessed in organisation, curricula, teaching strategies, etc., it is pertinent to seek systematic and up-to-data information on the significant correlates of a student achievement. It is appropriate, in this context, to consider factors affecting the academic achievement such as the student's socio-economic background, educational aspirations, etc. These factors are of utmost theoretical and practical importance in developing curricula, and designing educational programmes to suit the needs of students with varied backgrounds. Further, the study of these factors assumes special significance in view of their implications in respect of day-to-day curriculum planning on the part of the classroom teachers. Studies on the correlates of achievement, thus, need to be thoroughly examined with a view to derive maximum benefit from their findings for improved curricular development, efficient teaching, and better academic achievement.

SOCIO-ECONOMIC STATUS AND ACHIEVEMENT

At a time of lively appraisal of educational development, when many changes are being, witnessed in organisation, curricula and teaching techniques, it is pertinent to seek systematic and up-to-date information on the significant correlates of achievement. It is appropriate, in this context, to consider at once the factors affecting academic achievement such as the student's socio-economic background, personality traits, study habits, attitudes, medium of instruction and so on. As this study intends to identify the relationship between achievement and socio-economic status of students, let us look into the findings of the previous studies in this area.

Clark (1927) found that students whose parents had college education ranked higher in scholarship. Shuttleworth (1927) reported that the low-achieving group of students had strict religious home training.

Bear (1928) found parental occupation related to academic success. He reported that sons of farmers and businessmen ranked low in scholarship in comparison to those of artisans, salesmen and so on.

Austin (1964) found very high relationship between the tendency to drop out of college and parents' education and father's occupation. Sinha (1970), and Wig and Nagpal (1970) found low achievers represented more in occupational category agricultural or business.

Griffits (1926) found a close relationship between school grades and family size. Children from small families were found superior in school grades.

Havighurst (1964) contrasted achievement test performance of middle-class and lower-class children in 21 Chicago school districts. He found that 6th grade students in the seven districts with the highest average of socio-economic status ranged from a grade level to one year above grade level on reading and mathematics tests; in the seven lowest socio-economic status districts, the +1 scores clustered around one year below grade level.

Mishra, Dash and Padhi (1960) reported a correlation of 0.59 between home environment and school achievement whereas correlation of 0.31 between intelligence test scores and school achievement.

Menon (1973) found over-achievement and under-achievement are highly influenced by socio-economic status. Anand (1973) established relationship between socio-economic status and academic achievement even when the influence of intelligence of non-verbal and verbal type was partialled out. He also found that the impact of socio-economic environment was found to influence mental abilities and academic achievement.

Abraham (1974) found achievement level in English is associated with socio-economic status and Basavayya (1974) observed overall language achievement is influenced by the parental occupation and education.

A study on difficulties in learning English by Dewal (1974) revealed that effective teaching and learning are hampered by poor socio-economic background.

Bhaduri (1971) observed that the over-achievers showed higher scores on study habits, attitude to school, and religious-cultural background; the under-achievers on the contrary, tended to have a higher socio-economic status, a more congenial home condition and more of leisure time activities.

Lalithamma found that the achievement in mathematics was positively related to intelligence, study habits, interest in mathematics and socio-economic status. Correlation between socio-economic status and academic achievement as computed by Prakash Chandra (1975) was reported as positive and is supported by Homchandhuri (1980), Khanna (1980), Shukla (1984), Mehrotra (1986), Misra (1986), Singh (1986) and Rathaiah and Rao (1997) also.

Satyanandam (1969) highlighted two sub-aspects of socio-economic status, viz., educational level of parents and economic status of parents. According to him, the children of graduate parents performed far better than the children of matriculate parents.

Children of upper and lower, upper and middle economic strata only differed significantly on the variable of achievement. Chatterji, Mukherjee and Banerjee (1971) also found that parent's education level was directly related to the achievement of their children.

Khanna (1980) observed that the academic achievement of the children of educated parents, illiterate parents, and educated mothers was significantly correlated with the socio-economic status of the family. Menon (1972) also noticed that higher occupational and educational level of father, educational level of mother, family income and parental attention were related to high achievement.

Ojha (1979) concluded that the higher the socio-economic status, the better would be the academic achievement at high school level. Parental education, occupation, and income were also related with the educational achievement of both rural and urban boys of 9th class.

Choudhari (1975) expressed his opinion based on research that bright children normally come from families where parents having a higher level of education, were mostly engaged in professions requiring general knowledge, and had more income than the parents of dull students.

In Goswami's (1978) study, the scholastic achievement correlated highly with socio-economic status.

Goswami (1982) found a significant relationship between socio-economic status and reading interests and also between reading interests and academic achievement.

Jain (1981) states that the socio-economic level of the parents had a great impact on the pupil's achievement in Gujarati, social studies, science and mathematics. The pupils belonging to the upper socio-economic status achieved better than the pupils whose parents belonged to the middle and lower socio-economic levels, while the pupils from the middle socio-economic levels scored better than those with lower socio-economic status of the parents, in all the subjects. Academic achievement had a high positive correlation with socio-economic status.

Family background factors of college students, according to Siddiqui (1979) had positive relationship with the academic achievement of the students when the intelligence factor was held constant. Somasundaram observed that the variables which discriminated between the unselected groups of normal and under-achievers were socio-economic standards, introversion and family relations.

Griffits (1926) observed that within the family the older and the younger children tended to perform about equally well scholastically. Gupta (1982) found that birth order and the father's profession influenced the reading ability (in Hindi) of children studying in classes

III and IV. Chatterji, et. al (1971) concluded that the family size and the number of siblings were inversely related, especially in low intellectual level. Dave and Dave (1971) observed that the size of the family was not related to the academic achievement.

Dave and Dave (1971) noticed that a higher percentage of rank students belonged to homes having parental income, occupation and education, whereas a higher percentage of failed students belonged to homes having lower parental income, occupation and education.

In the study of Dhami (1974) the relationship between socio-economic status and academic achievement, though statistically significant, was not very high. Socio-economic status was moderately correlated with achievement in the study of Srivastava (1981). Sinha (1970) also observed only small differences on their parents, education and father's education. The socio-economic status of the pupil's parents was not significantly related to scholastic performance at Class VIII and Class IX but at Class X the pupils hailing from homes with higher socio-economic status performed better.

Nomzek (1940) reported that education of parents and their profession have no influence over the academic success of their children. But for the high ability group, children of servicemen excelled the children of businessmen, and the trend was reversed for the average and low intellectual groups.

Salunke (1979) found no relationship between socio-economic status and achievement. Bhat and Indiresan (1981) failed to draw definite conclusions regarding the differential performance of students belonging to different socio-economic backgrounds as the sample consisted mainly of students belonging to the backward class and low-income group.

Chatterji, Mukherjee and Banerjee (1971) concluded that the economic conditions of the family seemed to have no effect upon the scholastic achievement in all the intellectual ability groups. They also found that father's occupation was not consistently related to children's achievement. Desai (1979) observed no relationship between socio-economic status and achievement.

Shukla (1984), Mehrotra (1986), Misra (1986) and Singh (1986) showed a positive relationship between SES and academic achievement of the students. In the study conducted at the CIII. Srivastava and Ramaswamy (1986) found that the effect of SES on achievement in mathematics and social studies was significant. Dwivedi (1983) found that SES significantly affected achievement in Biology of higher secondary pre-medical students when taught through a linear programme.

In the study of Sarah (1983) it was found that the coefficient of correlation between achievement and SES was positive and significant when the effect of pupil's attitude towards science and towards science education were partialled out. Adolescents of high SES possessed high scholastic achievement according to Sharma (1984). In the Sontakey (1986), the high achievers had a high socio-economic status and they hailed from highly educated families. Trivedi (1987) showed that students belonging to upper socio-economic status groups showed better academic achievement than students belonging to lower socio-economic status groups. With reference to achievement in mathematics, Rajput (1984) established that socio-economic status of students affected their achievement. Though the high SES and average SES groups did not differ, the high SES and low SES groups did differ significantly on achievement in mathematics.

In the study by Das (1975) which was conducted in West Bengal, the socio-economic status was one of the primary factors responsible for low achievement in general science. Studying the relationship between certain psycho-sociological factors and achievement of student-teachers in teacher training institutes of Andhra Pradesh, Goplacharyulu (1984) showed that socio-economic status and caste influenced the total achievement as well as achievement in theory and practicals, taken separately, of the student-teachers.

Pandey (1981) and Puri (1984) studied the influence of environment as a factor to promote academic achievement among students. The former concluded that an urban atmosphere was more conducive to better achievement than a rural environment. The latter brought out that the effect of environmental facility on both general academic achievement and achievement in English language was significant.

The environment provided to the student by his home drew the attention of Grover (1979), Gaur (1982), Sarkar (1983), Lall (1984), Jagannadhan (1985), Maitra (1985), Paul (1986) and Trivedi (1987). A significant difference between high achievers and low achievers on the home variables—namely, educational environment, income, spatial environment, social background, provision of facilities, and parent-child relationship—was shown in Sarkar (1983). In the study by Maitra (1985) home environment was found to be an important variable which could cause under-achievement among the gifted. Studying the effects of home environment on the cognitive styles of students, Paul (1986) concluded that the factors of home environment, like recognition of the child's achievement, parental aspiration, forbearance for the child's wishes, parental affection, encouragement for initiative and freedom, etc., had positive and significant correlation with each of the four modes of cognitive styles studied. Grover (1979) indicated some influence of aspirations of father and mother over children's academic achievement. Gaur (1982) showed that birth order did not affect the speed of reading, comprehension and vocabulary of students. Trivedi (1987) found that parental attitude was significantly related to academic achievement. Lall (1984) showed that protective attitudes of parents was positively related to the academic success of boys. Jagannadhan's (1985) study indicates significant effect of home environment on academic achievement.

The environment provided at the learning place of students as a variable has been studied by Deshpande (1984), Doctor (1984) and Upadhyaya (1982). No specific trend of organizational climate was found to differentiate between the high and low achieving schools, according to Deshpande (1984). The study by Doctor (1984) indicated a relationship between classroom climate and academic achievement. Upadhyaya (1982) conducted the study on the tribal population of Bastar District in Madhya Pradesh. It was found that each of the three aspects of classroom environment—interpersonal relationships, goal orientation, and system maintenance and change—was significantly related to academic achievement.

Studies by Girija (1980), Mishra (1983), Malik (1984), Kamila (1985), Pandey Kalpalata (1985) and Verma (1985) have concentrated on samples of students who may be considered as slightly disadvantaged when compared to others. Kamila (1985) brought out a comparative picture between the achievement of students belonging to Harijan and Tribal Welfare Department high schools and those belonging to Education Department high schools in Orissa. The picture was in favour of the latter. In a study conducted in Uttar Pradesh by Verma (1985), the mean achievement of scheduled caste students was found to be significantly lower than that of tribal students and of students belonging to other castes. But, the study did not show any difference between the achievement of students belonging to scheduled tribes and those belonging to other castes. Patel (1987) attempted to compare the cognitive and personality differentials of the disadvantaged and advantaged secondary school children from Orissa. The study used a sample with an equal number of scheduled caste, scheduled tribe, and advantaged students. The findings revealed that the three groups differed significantly in their academic achievement. Mishra (1983) studied the effect of socio-economic background and culture on academic achievement of children. The sample included three sub-cultural groups, namely, the urban, the rural and the tribal. Each of these groups was further divided as socio-economically advantaged and socio-economically disadvantaged. The study showed that the advantaged children secured higher educational achievement scores than the disadvantaged children both in the urban and the rural sub-cultures. Among the disadvantaged children the tribals secured higher educational achievement scores than those of their urban and rural counterparts. Pandey Kalpalata (1985) showed that low deprived students performed better than high deprived students in certain subjects of study, namely, social studies, science and Hindi. Kathuria (1982) investigating a sample drawn from urban higher secondary schools of Bhilai and Raipur, found the relationship between scholastic achievement and global prolonged deprivation to be not significant. Girija (1980) explored predictor factors, both intellectual and non-intellectual, which contributed to the cumulative grade point average of advantaged and disadvantaged students of an agricultural university. Malik (1984) showed that first-generation learners had significantly lower academic achievement than the non-first generation learners.

Rathaiah (1993), Rathaiah and Bhaskara Rao (1997) have found a positive relationship between socio-economic status and achievement.

Socio-economic variables related students determined selection but were not relevant to subsequent academic performance.

Most of the studies in this category have attempted at replicating earlier studies taking different samples and by including different curricular subjects at various levels. We can't find a suitable research conducted taking sample from secondary schools situated in an educationally background state which is a necessity to identify the association of achievement and socio-economic status in this sample.

EDUCATIONAL ASPIRATIONS AND ACHIEVEMENT

Aspiration is a natural phenomenon of human life, and educational aspiration is no exception. Level of aspiration, the level of future performance in a task which an individual acts for himself knowing his past performance, is considered to play a significant role in scholastic achievement. Some psychologists define the level of aspiration as the level of future performance in a familiar task which an individual expects to achieve knowing his level of past performance in that task. In other occasion Mathis, Cotton and Sechrest (1970) opined that the level of aspiration is the degree of performance a person expects of himself in a specific situation.

Lewin (1926) assumed that the relation of the level of aspiration to the level of post performance at any time depends primarily on the relative strength of the following needs: (1) the need to keep the level of aspiration as high as possible, regardless of the level of performance, (2) the need to make the level of aspiration approximate the level of future performance as close as possible, and (3) the need to avoid failure, where failure is defined as a level of performance below the level of aspiration regardless of its absolute goodness and this need tends to drive the level of aspiration below the level of past performance.

It seems probable that the relative strength of these needs depends on the environmental factors but also on the personal factors of an individual. The person who habitually keeps his feet on the ground would be expected to keep his level of aspiration close to his level of past performance, while he whose head is in the clouds would keep his level of aspiration soaring high in any situation. A cautious individual would tend, as a rule, to keep his level of aspiration below his level of past performance and the ambitious person would typically set his level of aspiration high and persist high until he has raised his level of performance to meet it.

A mid degree of continued dissatisfaction is essential for providing motivation to an individual for continuously improving upon his past performances. If a state of complete satisfaction is arrived at, the process of further progress of the individual might come to a standstill. Therefore, for bettering the past achievement, a moderate degree of positive discrepancy between the level of achieved and the level of aspired is essential.

Level of aspiration is generally raised when performance equals the level of aspiration and lowered when performance falls below the level of aspiration. Jucknat (1937) studied the reaction of subjects to attainment or non-attainment of their levels of aspiration and found that their levels of aspiration and found that stronger the feeling of success the greater is the tendency to raise the level of aspiration and that the tendency to lower the aspiration is greater with a strong feeling of future. A commonly observed tendency of subjects is to maintain a moderate positive goal discrepancy.

Lewin (1944) reported that nearly all individuals of western culture, when first exposed to a level of aspiration situation, give initially a level of aspiration which is above the previous performance score, and under most conditions tend to keep the goal discrepancy positive.

Festinger (1942) observed that after an attainment of the level of aspiration there was 51 per cent rise, 41 per cent staying on the same level, and 8per cent lowering of the level of aspiration. After a non-attainment of the level of aspiration, it was raised in 7 per cent cases, stayed at the same level in 29 per cent cases and lowered in 64 per cent cases.

Menon (1972) found that job aspiration, educational aspiration and general ambition were strongly associated with high achievement, particularly in girls.

There are a few typical cases of equal importance. Sears (1940) observed that children with a past history of success showed very little variability in aspiration. Most of them maintained the typical small positive goal discrepancy. Children with past history of failure showed a much higher goal discrepancy and variability. Some had a very high positive goal discrepancies, they set their level of aspiration very much above their immediate past performance. Similar patterns of aspiration have been observed in later clinical studies of level of aspiration.

Studies of Gould and Kaplan (1940), Sears (1940), Holt (1942), Schultz and Ricciuti (1954) found no relationship between scholastic achievement and level of aspiration. Sharma (1979) also found that the level of aspiration did not influence academic achievement.

Muthayya concluded that high achievers and low achievers in scholastic do not significantly differ in aspiration level. Radha found that the level of aspiration has not been found to have significant bearing on academic achievement.

Gates and Jersild have stated that the level of aspiration is closely related to success and failure in college and that it may represent a goal or desire to improve the performance. Lowell and Atkinson (1953) reported a positive but low and not significant relationship between level of aspiration and achievement motive among high and low achievers. Kuppuswamy informed that the achievement in school is closely related to the level of aspiration. Shukla (1973) observed that the level of aspiration determines the limits of academic achievement to some extent. Hussain (1977) concluded that the academic performance of the group showing moderate goal discrepancy was better than that of the groups showing either high or low goal discrepancy, implying a curvilinear relationship between the level of aspiration and academic performance.

Bryan and Locke concluded that academic performance can be increased by suggesting what level a person should aspire for. Sears

(1940) and Rotter (1943) have found that groups with a history of poor academic achievement had higher average goal discrepancy scores than groups with a history of high achievement.

Ramkumar observed a strong association between achievement and goal discrepancy and pointed out that achievement is higher with a decline in goal discrepancy scores.

Rathaiah (1993) and Rathaiah and Bhaskara Rao (1997) found a close relationship between achievement and educational aspirations.

With the above review of the available related research, one does not come across many research reports on the level of aspirations in relation to academic achievement. Some of the researchers have found no relationship between level of aspiration and scholastic achievement, whereas some have found them to be positively related. As some researchers have reported, there seems to exist a negative relationship between achievement and level of aspiration. None of the researchers reported above studied the relationship between level of aspiration and achievement, at tenth class level which is a crucial stage in the educational system.

3

DESIGN OF THE STUDY

Design is the heart of every research activity. For this study, a study of the following aspects has been discussed.

Research Procedures followed: This includes the operational definitions of different terms used, the hypotheses that are framed for testing and the rationale of the formulated hypotheses.

Selection of the Sample: This includes the sampling techniques used, the reasons for selection of a particular sampling technique, and the selection of sample according to variables.

Selection of Tools: This includes the selection of suitable tools for collection of data, description of tools selected, testing their suitability for the present study, and the procedure followed in administering the tools to collect the data required for the present study.

The present study is divided into the following areas to study them in depth in a specific and concrete way. The areas are—socio-economic status, educational aspirations, achievement in Social Studies and the relationship between socio- economic status and achievement in Social Studies and educational aspirations and achievements in Social Studies.

The following five variables are selected in each of the sub-areas of the study taking the objectives into consideration. They are; 1. residential versus non-residential secondary schools, 2. private versus government secondary schools, 3. urban versus rural secondary schools, 4. Telugu medium versus English medium secondary schools, and 5. boys and girls.

After specifying the objectives, areas and variables, the tools to be used for the collection of data are finalized. To measure the major aspects of the study, Socio-Economic Scale standardized by Beena Shah was used to estimate the socio-economic status of the students of secondary schools. To measure the Educational Aspirations the Scale of S.K. Saxena was adopted to identify the educational aspirations of the students. A part from the above two areas, i.e., the Socio-economic Status and the educational aspirations, the average marks of the students in their quarterly, half-yearly, pre-public and public examination in Social Studies was also taken as their academic achievement. The Socio-Economic Status scale, and Educational Aspirations Scale are translated into Telugu also. The tools were made ready for use in this study after verifying the validity and reliability.

The population of the present study consists of the students of tenth class studying in secondary schools. From this population, a representative sample had to be selected. After a detailed study of different techniques of sampling, the stratified sampling technique was found to be the most suitable one and was used for the collection of data. A sample of 700 students was selected through this stratified sampling technique by taking the different variables under study into consideration. The data were collected personally from the sample and the authorities of the secondary schools in West Godavari district.

Hypotheses were formulated for testing the present study and analysis is presented in the forthcoming pages of this chapter.

Before going into the details of the sample, sampling techniques and tools, it will be worthwhile if we discuss the operational definitions of key terms used in the present study which will enlighten the characteristics involved in each term.

OPERATIONAL DEFINITIONS OF KEY TERMS

The present study, *"A Study of Socio-Economic Status and Educational Aspirations of Secondary School Students in relation to their*

Achievement in Social Studies", is having some key terms which are to be clearly defined to avoid misunderstanding and hence herewith are discussed and defined.

ACHIEVEMENT

Achievement in an educational institution may be taken to mean any desirable learning that is observed in the student. Since the word desirable implies a value judgement, it is obvious that a particular learning may be referred to as achievement or otherwise depending on whether it is considered desirable or not. Understood in this way, any behaviour that is learned may come within the scope of achievement. Achievement, according to Smith (1969), and Spence and Helmrich (1983), is the task-oriented behaviour that allows the individual's performance to be evaluated internally or externally that involves the individual in competing with others, or that otherwise involves some standard of excellence.

There is no gain saying the fact that learning is not limited to mere acquisition of information, it also includes attitudes, interests, values, etc. Modern personality characteristics of the individual are learned. Therefore, the acquisition of desirable characteristics is as much an achievement as is knowledge of the principles of science or facts, world history or language and literature. Although achievement is used in this broad sense it is customary for schools and colleges to be concerned to a great extent with the development of knowledge, understanding and acquisition of skills. In other words, the learning which educational intimations concern themselves with, is predominantly intellectual. This may be in part owing to the fact that in the intellectual field the teacher can be relatively more certain of achieving the objectives he had set for himself than in other areas or domains.

The teacher or the institution has certain objectives which are often stated as the development of desirable characteristics of personality. Though this is undoubtedly a worthy goal, it is doubtful whether anything beyond the most superficial change could be obtained with the small number of hours contact between the teacher and the taught in the college. Thus in practice, the objectives are necessarily restricted to the imparting of various types of subject-matter knowledge.

Academic achievement is related to the acquisition of principles and generalizations and the capacity to perform efficiently, certain manipulations of objects, symbols and ideas. Assessment of academic performance has been largely confirmed to the evaluation in terms of information, knowledge and understanding. It is universally accepted that the acquisition of factual data is not an end in itself but an individual who has received education should show evidence of having understood them. But, for obvious reasons the examinations are largely confirmed to the measurement of the amount of information which students have acquired.

Wood and Learned (1938) concluded from their well known Pennsylvania study that education was unavoidably intellectual in which knowledge was the dominating feature of educational outcomes. It is perhaps the only accepted basis of promotion of fulfilment or requirements for degree or diploma. It is the actual or assumed possession of knowledge that counts either for admission into a class or course. Educational measurements may be made with reference to either the aims or the results of education or both. The acquisition of knowledge consists of the registering of data or the making of a datum either more definite and indelible or meaningful. This conception of acquiring knowledge assumes that the student is an active organism in a stimulus-response situation, that the student interprets his experience, that he shows evidence of having registered and interpreted the datum by his appropriate response to it and that in future situations he will be guided by prior experience. Understood in this way measurement can be in terms of subject matter and this does not claim to minimize the importance of the other aspects of education.

Examinations in one form or another were employed by people ever since the days of early civilizations. Paul F. Cressey, a sociologist, attributes the remarkable stability of the old Chinese civilization among other things to her highly organized examination system. Examinations are not only used extensively, they vitally affect and determine the careers of students. From the earliest times teachers have examined as well as taught. Some kind of measurement or evaluation seems suitable in education and it is an essential part of the teaching learning process.

Achievement in terms of subject matter is conventionally assessed in our institutions by employing a system of marks or grades. It has been strongly argued that marks are necessary for effective teaching learning. Trabue (1926) felt that, for classification, guidance and evidence of effort, marks are necessary. A Committee of the Principals of California listed the purposes of marks as the indication of the degree of mastery of subject matter and the prediction of future success. Madsen (1930) points out that marks set goals and motivate the students. Symonds (1927) listed among the purposes of marks the following: incitement of study, promotion of competition, determination of promotion, assistance in education and vocational guidance, awarding credits and honors. It is universally accepted that marks serve as the basis of classification and certification, motivation and measurement of educational performance.

The purpose of the study is on the basis of knowledge acquired on achievement. The word achievement denotes that the marks acquired by the students in their examinations.

SOCIO-ECONOMICS STATUS

Society is an organization of interacting people whose activities center around a set of common goals and who tend to share common beliefs, attitudes and modes of action. It is obvious that the society limits the activities of the individuals, by setting up standards which they have to follow and maintain. Thus society is a system of usages and procedures and involves authority as well as natural aid. There are many groups of people doing different kinds of work and following different kinds of norms in a complex and pluralistic society. In many societies, stratification is characteristic feature. The phenomena involved in social stratification are chiefly palterned interaction and stratum consciousness. Each status has free interactions with the members of that stratum and restricted interactions with members belonging to the strata superior to it, as well as with those inferior to it. This is because there are different styles of life in different strata or society with respect to education, occupation, possession, recreations and manners.

These characteristics are there in the social life whether it is organized on the basis of caste or class. These differences are based on upbringing, education, occupation and income. While in the Indian caste system the strata are 'closed' groups, in the modern class system the strata are 'open' groups with opportunities for social mobility. Another significant characteristic of the so-called casteless and classless societies, like the American or Soviet societies is that the large majority consists of what the Amercians call the middle class and what the Soviets call the working class.

The concept of stratification is closely linked with the concept of status. In a broad way it may be asserted that social status accrues to a person on the basis of the possession by him, of the characteristics valued by his society. Thus, the term status is meaningful in every kind of society. Status may be based on strength and skill or on the basis of the possession of land and wealth or on the basis of education and knowledge and so on. Every society, whether rural or urban, whether industrial or agricultural, has a status system. People are recognized as differing in status, some being perceived as of superior status and some as inferior of status.

The objective characteristics most frequently used are education, occupation and income. This is why it is called socio-economic status.

EDUCATIONAL ASPIRATIONS

Left to their own devices, most children would live in the present and let the future take care of itself. But they are not left to their own devices. Even before they enter school, parents, relatives and family friends ask children what they are planning to do when they are grown up. Most of the adults regard a child who says. "I want to be the Prime Minister of India" or " I am going to be a doctor or an engineer", as ambitious, and as courageous.

In a culture which provides vast opportunities for its members to be and to achieve what they want, it is understandable that children at an early age would be subjected to pressures to create aspirations for the future. Aspirations, it is believed, motivate children to take advantage of the opportunities parents and society provide.

Social pressures to plan for the future are reinforced by competition with members of the peer group in play and school or college work. As the students compare what they can do with what their peers can do, it adds new meanings to their aspirations and puts new emphasis on the creation of aspirations that are both ego satisfying and admired by members of the social group. Thus, forming aspirations become an important area of creativity in students.

To the layman, aspiration is synonymous with ambition. It suggests that the person is not only planning personal betterment but is carrying out this plan in real life. In the strictest sense, as used by the psychologist, ambition means a desire for honour, power or attainment. By contrast, aspiration means longing for what is above one, with advancement as its goal. Aspiration emphasizes the desire to improve or to rise above one's present status.

If aspiration and ambition were synonymous, and meant honourable attainment, people would be satisfied if their achievements were recognized and applauded by others. Children, for example, would be satisfied if their parents or relatives praised them for the houses they built in sand or with blocks, or for the drawings they made. If, on the other hand, the desire to improve or to have what is above one is taken into consideration, children would not necessarily be satisfied with their houses or drawings just because their parents praised them. Instead, they would be satisfied only if their houses or drawings met with the standards they set for themselves. This distinction is important because it helps to explain much of the dissatisfied children—as well as adolescents and adults - experience in connection with their achievements and why, as a result, aspirations play such a large role in personal and social adjustments.

Aspirations are influenced by personal factors like—wishes for what individuals want to achieve; personal interests, which influence the areas of aspirations; past experience with success strengthening aspirations and failures weakening them; the personality pattern, which influences both the kind and strength of aspirations; personal values, which determine what aspirations are important; sex, with boys aspiring higher than girls; socio-economic status, with those of the middle and upper groups aspiring higher than those of the lower groups; and racial background, with those of minority group status often aspiring unrealistically high as a form of compensation.

Aspirations are also influenced by the environmental factors such as perental ambitions, which are higher for first-born than later-born children; social expectetions which emphasize that those who are successful in one area can be successful in all areas if they wish; peer pressures to set aspirations in areas important to the peer group; group emphasis on sex appropriateness of aspirations; cultural traditions which hold that all people can achieve anything they wish if they try hard enough; social values, which vary with the area of achievement; mass media, which encourages achievement aspirations; social rewards for high achievement and social neglect or rejection for low achievement, competition which siblings and peers view in the hope of showing one's superiority over them.

Aspirations, say for achievement or so, are influenced more by environmental factors than by personal factors. Some environmental influences encourage the development of immediate aspirations and some encourage remote aspirations; foster positive aspirations while others foster negative aspirations; some motivate the individual to be realistic and other unrealistic. In early childhood, before children are old enough to know what their abilities, interests and values are, their aspirations are largely shaped by their environments. As children grow older and are more aware of their abilities and interests, personal factors have a greater influence, but many of their aspirations are still environmental in origin.

Aspirations vary not only in strength but, even more important, in kind. They may be positive or negative. In the former, the emphasis is on winning success or doing better than one has done before, while in the latter, the emphasis is on avoiding failure. Immediate aspirations are goals the person sets for the immediate future—today, tomorrow, next week, or next month—while remote aspirations are goals set for the future. Childhood aspirations are likely to be unrealistic because knowledge and experiences at this age are limited. Adulthood aspirations may be realistic and or idealistic.

Aspirations may be of educational, vocational, professional, social, sexual, economical etc. Educational aspirations include courses such as medicine and engineering, science and technology, civil services, social sciences to sculpture, tailoring to trade, clerk to corps, general officer to educational administrator, and so on.

SOCIO—ECONOMIC STATUS SCALE

The social status accrues to a man on the basis of the possession by him, of the characteristics valued by his society. The status may be based on strength and skill or on the basis of the possession of land and wealth or on the basis of education and knowledge and so on. Every society, whether rural or urban, whether industrial or agricultural, has a status system. People are different from one another in their status. Some are known for their superior status and others for inferior status.

Measurement of socio-economic status is a major operation in almost all researches related to social concept. According to Linton the whole concept of status has emerged in terms of social differentiation. Socio- economic status scale preparators have incorporated variables like family size, education, occupation, social position, case, land ownership, social participation and possessions. But to identify the correct categories and minimize the perceptual content in socio-economic status for its accurate measurement, limited variables like caste, occupation, education, income, possession and social participation are being used in socio-economic status scales.

Based on the information of the socio-economic status scale, the socio-economic status can be classified into five categories, viz., upper status, upper middle status, middle status, lower middle status and lower status.

The present selected socio-economic status scale is intended to identify the socio-economic status to the students of junior colleges.

EDUCATIONAL ASPIRATIONS SCALE

It is the human nature to aspire for something after something. Without having proper aspirations one cannot rise high in any field and earn prestige and fulfil his needs.

The aspirations range from social, cultural to technological and educational. The educational aspirations, include becoming doctors, engineers, lawyers, professors, collectors, police officials, technicians, scientists, administrators, etc. The higher the aspirations, the greater is the ability of the students.

The scale of the educational aspirations selected for this study is meant for the students studying in senior intermediate in junior colleges.

ACHIEVEMENT TEST

The term achievement is often understood in terms of a student's scores in a certain test. If, for instance, a student is tested in two school subjects, say English and Mathematics and in one subject he gets 50 per cent marks while in other 70 per cent marks, it is understood that his achievement in English in which he gets 50 per cent marks is not better than that in Mathematics in which he gets 70 per cent marks. This is a loose way of understanding the concept of achievement. More intelligently understood, achievement means one's learning attainments, accomplishments, proficiencies, etc. Achievement is directly related to a pupil's growth and development in educational situations where learning and teaching are intended to go on simultaneously. Achievement involves aptitude for learning, readiness for learning and opportunity for learning. Besides these factors, it also involves health and physical fitness, motivation, special aptitude, and emotional balances.

Freeman defines a test of educational achievement as a test designed to measure knowledge, understanding, skills in a specified subject or group of subjects. Thus according to him, an educational achievement test measures an individual's knowledge and understanding or skills in a particular branch of knowledge. Further,

Freeman is of the view that through educational achievement test, it is possible to ascertain how much a person knows after receiving education or training in a particular branch of knowledge. The standardized achievement tests are used to determine the degree of achievement in a specific subject matter. Achievement tests attempt to measure what an individual has learned and what is his or her present level of performance.

Anastasi has discussed the various uses of achievement tests—achievement tests are used to ascertain the attainment of minimum performance standards. In other words, an achievement test is to find out whether an individual has attained the required ability in a given field of knowledge or activity. Another important use of an achievement test is to be seen when there is a need for selecting candidates in regard to certain jobs or courses.

An achievement test is also used for purposes of guidance and counselling. It has found useful in remedial teaching programmes as well as in determining the class to which a student should be admitted into. Administration of these tests at regular intervals is helpful to the teachers in knowing the kinds of difficulties faced by the pupils in learning. Finally it may be stated that the achievement test may be used as an aid in the evaluation of teaching, the importance of instructional techniques, and the revision of curriculum content.

Residential Secondary Schools

In the Residential secondary schools students should stay on in the school campus with their teachers instead of coming daily from their houses. So they spend all their time either on the school premises or in the hostels, and pursue studies under the constant supervision of teachers. Such schools were considered residential secondary schools.

Non-Residential Secondary Schools

The students of these schools will only be in the school campus during instructional hours and spend their remaining time at home or at other places. Such schools were considered non-residential secondary schools.

Private Secondary Schools

The schools managed by private organizations or persons, either partially or totally, were included in private secondary schools. The Government recognized and Government aided schools were also included under private secondary schools.

Government Secondary Schools

The schools under the sole management of Government were included in this category. This consists of the secondary schools managed by the Government of Andhra Pradesh and the Societies under the control of the Government of Andhra Pradesh, such as A.P. Residential, A.P. Social Welfare, Government schools, etc.

Rural Secondary Schools

The schools located in rural areas were considered as rural schools. A rural area should have a population below five thousand with 75 per cent of its population engaged in agricultural activities.

Urban Secondary Schools

The schools located in an urban area were considered as urban schools. The urban area should be municipal corporation with 75 per cent of its working population engaged in non-agricultural pursuits.

Telugu Medium Secondary Schools

The schools which impart instruction in Telugu medium were considered Telugu Medium Schools.

English Medium Secondary Schools

The schools which provide instruction in English medium were considered English Medium Schools.

VARIABLES OF THE STUDY

Variables are a necessary requisite for any worthwhile research for the purpose of comparison. For the present study the following variables are considered. They are: residential versus non-residential, private versus government, rural versus urban, Telugu medium versus English medium and boys versus girls. The rationale for choosing the above stated variables is discussed hereunder.

Residential versus Non-Residential Secondary Schools

The residential schools are supposed to be in better position in all aspects when compared with non-residential schools. The students of the residential schools stay in the college itself without going home after the regular classroom teaching learning activities. They stay with their teachers all the time, except for a few hours, and study and clear off their doubts immediately either in the classroom or during study hours. Contrary to this, the students of non-residential schools stay outside the school except 6 or 7 hours, and spend their remaining time at their own will and interest. The students interested in studies usually get some doubts during their study at home, but they have to wait for quite a long time to clear them off. The delay in getting them cleared off sometimes leads to frustration or carelessness. This teaching learning aspect will definitely play an important role in the achievement of students.

The infrastructure, the laboratory and library facilities will also be better in residential schools. In Andhra Pradesh, the Government residential schools were started offering the best education to the students by providing facilities conducive to the progress of each and every student. The same way is followed by the private managements which established a large number of private residential schools excelling in results and catching state ranks. The intelligent students will always be in a better position, as they are not mixed up with the lesser intelligent students, which is a practice in non-residential schools generally.

Considering the above facts, the students of residential and non-residential secondary schools were taken into consideration to study the achievement of the students.

Private Versus Government Secondary Schools

The reputation of private schools is generally far superior when compared with that of the government schools. In private schools the students are exposed to better conditions and better study atmosphere. The laboratories and libraries will be better. If better facilities are not provided in private schools the parents will question the authorities concerned as they pay higher fees for their wards.

The quality of teaching is also supposed to be better in private schools. The teachers take more interest in teaching in private schools as they are always or to some extent in the fear of either losing their jobs or immediately being questioned by the managements about the quality of their teaching.

Since the standard of teaching and the physical facilities are supposed to be different in private and government schools, the achievement of the students will be different and hence this variable is taken into consideration for this study.

Rural School Versus Urban Secondary Schools

The urban schools are well equipped in many aspects when compared with rural schools. The buildings, the libraries, the laboratories, the teaching staff, the educational atmosphere, the competitive spirit, etc., will always be better in urban schools than in rural schools. So a comparison between rural and urban school students will bring out the difference in the level of socio-economic status, educational aspirations and achievement in Social Studies.

Telugu Medium Versus English Medium Secondary Schools

Usually people feel that there may not be much more difference between the students of Telugu Medium and English Medium. But many studies in various fields proved that the students studying in their mother tongue [here in this study is Telugu] score better because they understand anything without any hindrance. For those who are studying in English Medium (a foreign language in the study) there may be a communication gap or delay in understanding a phenomenon owing to language hindrance. As there will be a gap between these two cases in terms of understanding and use of knowledge, there may exist a difference in the level of educational aspirations and achievement. Usually, as the middle or high socio-economic status students pursue their education in English medium by paying the high fee, they may develop high educational aspirations and achieve well in exams.

Boys Versus Girls

Sex is taken as a variable to see if there is any significant difference between boys and girls in their achievement. In olden days, boys were educated and the girls were restricted to their kitchens by their adult community. Times have changed and the adults recognized the importance of women education. In the words of our late Prime Minister Pandit Jawaharlal Nehru, 'if you educate a man you educate only one person, if you educate a woman you educate the entire family'. In due course, women education gained importance and many parents are encouraging their daughters to pursue higher education, even allowing them to go abroad. Women are also showing excellence in all fields and their presence is felt almost in all fields.

As the physiological conditions, exposure to society, education and other aspects of girls and boys vary differently, there may be a significant difference in the performance. The boys may be exposed to the society to a larger extent, but the girls spend most of their times in going through books or helping their parents at home. These factors will show their influence on their mental development and performance.

HYPOTHESES OF THE STUDY

Hypotheses are the tentative conclusions intended for verification. The hypotheses were formulated in small form as "A Null hypotheses states that there is no significant difference or relationship between two or more parameters". The hypotheses and their rationale were explained in the following pages.

Socio-Economic Status

Society is an organization of interacting people whose activities centre around a set of common goals and who tend to share common beliefs, attitudes and modes of action (Kuppuswamy, 1980). It is obvious that the society limits the activities of the individuals by setting up standards which they have to follow and maintain. Thus society is a system of usages and procedures and involves authority as well as mutual aid. There are many groups of people doing different kinds of norms in a complex and a pluralistic society.

Since the society in India, as elsewhere, consists of different classes, it is but natural for the researchers to think of the conditions and influences for the scholastic achievement.

The following are the hypotheses formulated in this area:

Hypothesis 1

The secondary school students do not possess high socio-economic status.

Hypothesis 1 A

There is no significant difference in the level of socio-economic status of residential and non-residential secondary school students.

Hypothesis 1 B

There is no significant difference in the level of socio-economic status of rural and urban secondary school students.

Hypothesis 1 C

There is no significant difference in the level of socio-economic status of private and government secondary school students.

Hypothesis 1 D

There is no significant difference in the level of socio-economic status of Telugu medium and English medium secondary school students.

Hypothesis 1 E

There is no significant difference in the level of socio-economic status of boys and girls.

Educational Aspirations

Aspiration means longing for what is above one, with advancement as its goal (Hurlock, 1978). Aspirations emphasize the desire to improve or to raise above one's present status. Educational aspirations help the students in achieving the set goals in the field of education.

Educational aspirations are influenced by personal factors such as wishes, interests, past experiences, personality pattern, personal values, sex, socio-economic status, etc., and environmental factors such as parental ambitions, social expectations, peer pressures, group ambitions, cultural aspects, social values, social rewards etc. As the educational aspirations play a major role in deciding the educational performance of students, it was decided to study the educational aspirations of secondary school students.

The following were the hypotheses formulated in this area:

Hypothesis 2

The secondary school students do not possess higher educational aspirations.

Hypothesis 2 A

There is no significant difference in the level of educational aspirations of residential and non-residential secondary school students.

Hypothesis 2 B

There is no significant difference in the level of educational aspirations of rural and urban secondary school students.

Hypothesis 2 C

There is no significant difference in the level of educational aspirations of private and government secondary school students.

Hypothesis 2 D

There is no significant difference in the level of educational aspirations of Telugu medium and English medium secondary school students.

Hypothesis 2 E

There is no significant difference in the level of educational aspirations of boys and girls.

Achievement In Social Studies

Achievement has a paramount importance, particularly in the present socio- economic and cultural contexts, and great emphasis is placed on achievement right from the beginning of the formal education. It is a task-oriented behaviour that allows the individual's performance to be evaluated according to some internally or externally imposed criterion, that involves some standard of excellence.

Achievement is related to the acquisition of principles and generalizations and the capacity to perform efficiently, certain manipulations of objects, symbols and ideas. Assessment of achievement has been largely conformed to the evaluation in terms of knowledge and understanding. It is universally accepted that the acquisition of factual data is not an end in itself but that an individual who has received education should show the evidence of having understood them. But, for obvious reasons the examinations are largely confirmed to the measurement of the amount of information by students.

Achievement in terms of subject matter is conventionally assessed in our institutions by employing a system of marks or grades, and it has been strongly argued that marks of grades, and it has been strongly argued that marks are necessary for effective teaching learning. Marks also set goals and motivate the students. It is universally accepted that marks serve as the basis of classification and certification, measurement and analysis of educational achievement.

The following were the hypotheses formulated in this area:

Hypothesis 3

The secondary school students do not possess high achievement in social studies.

Hypothesis 3 A

There is no significant difference in the level of achievement in social studies or residential and non-residential secondary school students.

Hypothesis 3 B

There is no significant difference in the level of achievement in social studies of rural and urban secondary school students.

Hypothesis 3 C

There is no significant difference in the level of achievement in social studies of private and government secondary school students.

Hypothesis 3 D

There is no significant difference in the achievement in social studies of Telugu medium and English medium secondary school students.

Hypothesis 3 E

There is no significant difference in the achievement in social studies of boys and girls.

Socio-Economic Status and Achievement

The central characteristic of a society is that it is an organization of interacting people whose activities center around a set of common goals and who tend to share common beliefs, attitudes and modes of action. It is startified with different categories of status. Social status is accrued to a person on the basis of possession by him, land and wealth, strength and skill, education and knowledge, and so on. The objective characteristics mostly used are education, occupation and income.

A set of potentially influential factors for student achievement are generally categorized as being associated either with home or school environment. It should, however, be noted that the distinction is more of convenience than of explanatory value. For one, the characteristics of the college one attends tend to vary according to one's home background. For another, it is not themselves but in relation to his experiences at college that many of the distinctive characteristics of a student's home environment may influence his academic performance.

Since the society in India consists of different classes, it is but natural for the researchers to think of the extent to which home conditions influence the academic achievement of the students. Sudane (1973) and Reddy (1973) found no significant correlations between socio-economic status and academic achievements. But Satyanandam (1969), Menon, (1973) Anand (1973), Abraham (1974), Basavayya (1974), Dave and Dave (1971), Chandra (1975), Chatterji, et.al. (1971) , Gupta (1982), Rathaiah and Rao (1997), Salunke (1979), Khanna (180), Gupta (1982) and many other studies established a positive relationship between performance and socio-economic status of the family.

In an early study Sherman and Key (1932) tested children from several hollows in the Blue Ridge Mountains approximately one hundred miles from Washington, D.C. Life in this cultural setting was characterized by an extreme degree of poverty, low literacy, poor educational facilities, and isolation from other communities. Not surprisingly, then, the children achieved less than average scores, and performance was related to the cultural level of the individual hollows.

With this it seems clearly that there is relationship between achievement and socio-economic status. But here we wish to see this relationship in secondary school students.

The following hypotheses were formulated in this area:

Hypothesis 4

There is no significant association between socio-economic status and achievement in social studies in residential secondary schools.

Hypothesis 4 A

There is no significant association between socio-economic status and achievement in social studies in residential and non-residential secondary schools.

Hypothesis 4 B

There is no significant association between socio-economic status and achievement in social studies in rural and urban secondary school students.

Hypothesis 4 C

There is no significant association between socio-economic status and achievement in social studies in private and government secondary school students.

Hypothesis 4 D

There is no significant relation between socio-economic status and achievement in social studies in Telugu medium and English medium secondary school students.

Hypothesis 4 E

There is no significant association between socio-economic status and achievement in social studies in boys and girls.

Educational Aspirations and Achievement

Aspiration is a longing for what is above one, with advancement as its goal. It emphasizes the desire to improve or to rise above one's present status. It is a measure of one's intentional disposition, an important element of long range behaviour. It is necessary to have knowledge of the aspirational level of an individual, both from educational and from guidance point of view.

Unemployment, underemployment and unsuitable employment are some of the major problems of the educated youth. Educational institutions are charged with the responsibility of developing vocational behaviours which may solve some of these problems. Right type of educational and vocational choices therefore have come to occupy a central place in the life of students. Educational aspirations keep the student on the track of hard work to achieve the set goal. Depending on the social status, interests, capabilities, facilities, etc., the educational aspirations vary in a wide range from individual to individual.

Under this area, educational aspirations and achievement, the following hypotheses were framed.

Hypothesis 5

There is no significant association between educational aspirations and achievement in social studies in secondary school students.

Hypothesis 5 A

There is no significant association between educational aspirations and achievement in social studies in residential and non-residential secondary school students.

Hypothesis 5 B

There is no significant association between educational aspirations and achievement in social studies in rural and urban secondary school students.

Hypothesis 5 C

There is no significant association between educational aspirations and achievement in social studies in private and government secondary school students.

Hypothesis 5 D

There is no significant association between educational aspirations and achievement in social studies in Telugu medium and English medium secondary school students.

Hypothesis 5 E

There is no significant association between educational aspirations and achievement in social studies in boys and girls.

SELECTION OF SAMPLE

After specifying the variables of the present study, consideration was given to whether the entire population is to be made the subject for data collection or a particular group is to be selected as representative of the whole population. The 'entire population' here refers to all the tenth class students of Andhra Pradesh.

Of the two techniques, the second one, namely, the selection of a group as a representative of the whole population was found to be more convenient and suitable. This technique leads to a considerable saving of time, effort and finance. The number of students selected is small, and so it is possible to make a detailed and intensive study. This generally leads to more accurate and reliable results. As this sampling technique has many advantages, it was selected for the collection of data.

In any social research, various methods are utilized for selection and drawing of samples. After a detailed study of all these methods, and considering the variables selected for the research work, the stratified sampling method was found to be most suitable.

In the stratified sampling method, the entire population is divided into smaller homogeneous groups or strata, and then the sample is selected within each group. Every sampling unit in the population is placed in one of the strata prior to the selection of the sample so that the sum of the strata is identical with the population.

Stratified sampling method has certain merits and advantages as a technique of sampling. Auckoff has rightly said that 'stratified sampling enables the researcher to make a comparison of properties of the strata as well as to estimate population characteristics.

In this stratified sampling method, the investigator has greater control over the selection of the sample when compared with random sampling. In random sampling, although every group has a chance of being selected and included in the sample, there is every possibility, and sometimes it does happen, that certain important groups are left unrepresented. But in stratified sampling method no important group is likely to be left out.

Stratified sampling method is the ideal one when comparison between different variables has to be made. For example, if comparison has to be made between residential and non-residential or private and government school students, it would be very difficult to select the required number of units through any other method of sampling. If any other method is used, the problem of bias and prejudice creeps in.

Replacement of units is also possible in the stratified sampling method. Normally if a particular unit is not accessible to a study, it is difficult to replace it by another, but in this method it is possible. Stephen states that 'stratification automatically brings about a replacement of persons lost to the sample, by persons of the same stratum, thus partly correcting the bias that would result if there were no replacement of losses. As the entire population is divided into particular strata it is easy and convenient to replace an inaccessible case by an accessible one.

In this stratified sampling method, much depends on the stratification process. The following precautions were taken while stratifying the population: the variables involved in the study were taken note of; care was taken to see that each stratum in the universe was large enough in size so that selection of items could be made on random basis; the strata formed were definite and clear cut; each stratum was free from influence of the other; that there was no overlapping.

Before actually selecting the sample, certain fundamental principles were considered to make the sample scientific and clear-cut.

Firstly, the 'universe' was clearly defined. In the technical phraseology of research, the whole population out of which the samples are selected is known as the ''universe'. For the present research work, the universe included all the students of tenth class studying in secondary schools of Andhra Pradesh. The study was limited to a particular geographical area to facilitate appropriate sample selection and to avoid bias and prejudice.

According to the *second principle*, decision has to be made about the units of the sample. A unit of sample may be a house, a family, a group of individuals or a single individual. A good unit should possess the following characteristics:

(a) ***Clarity***: The unit should be clearly defined in unambiguous terms. This would make the study easy and efficient. For the present research work, a sampling unit was defined as a pupil of tenth class studying in any secondary school in Andhra Pradesh;

(b) ***Suitability***: A good unit should be well suited to the problem under study. Since the problem is related to the secondary school students, the unit selected is well suited to the problem;

(c) ***Accessibility***: The unit selected should be easily accessible to the researcher. If the units selected are difficult to reach and if we fail to make use of them, the study would be vitiated. The selected sampling unit, i.e., a tenth class student is easily accessible since the researcher could approach in any secondary school.

The *third principle* to be considered while selecting a sample is the availability and preparation of the source list. This is an important factor that makes representative selection possible. A source list is the list which contains the names of the units of the universe from which the sample may be selected. It may exist even before the beginning of the project or it may be prepared afresh by the investigator herself. Without a source list, study through the sampling method is not possible. For the present research work, a source list, consisting of the names of secondary schools of West Godavari district, was used. Care was taken to see that the source list was up-to-date and valid and that there was no repetition of names of the schools. This source list was found to be relevant and suitable because it included the colleges since the study deals with the secondary school students.

Besides considering these principles, it is extremely important to think about the size of the sample to be selected. If the sample is either very small or very large, it will make the study difficult and also make the results untenable. According to Parten, 'an optimum sample in survey is the one which fulfils the requirements of effective representativeness, reliability and flexibility. The sample should be small enough to avoid intolerable sampling error'. The size of the sample for the present research work was decided after considering the following factors.

(a) The nature of the study-since an intensive study was planned, a very large number of samples were not selected. In case of an intensive study, very large number of samples are not so useful as they involve huge consumption of the resources. A smaller sample is found to be convenient.

(b) The size and the selection of the samples are also influenced by the nature of the universe. If the universe is homogeneous, even a small sized sample may yield dependable and required results. If the universe is heterogeneous, small sized samples may not be useful. In case of the present study, the heterogeneous universe was split into smaller homogeneous strata or groups and the samples were selected from the strata. A sample was selected from each of these two groups.

(c) The investigator needs to determine the number of the groups to be formed. In case the number of groups proposed are large, the size of the samples shall have to be large so that every group should be of proper size and suit the requirements of the study. In case the number of groups proposed are small, every small-sized samples can fulfil the requirement. In the case of the present study, the number of groups into which the universe was divided are girls and boys, private and government secondary schools, residential and non-residential secondary schools, Telugu medium and English medium schools, and rural and urban schools. Since the number of groups are more, a reasonable large sample was selected from each of these groups.

(d) Practical considerations and accuracy also play a vital role in determining the size of the sample. Every study is guided by certain practical considerations such as time, resources, accessibility of the data, etc. Generally, it is believed that a large-sized sample is more representative and generally produces accurate results. This, of course, depends upon the technique of sampling used. If the technique is scientific, even small-sized samples can produce dependable and accurate results. While selecting the size of the sample for the present study, practical considerations like the availability of resources and time were taken into consideration. Care was taken to make the sample-selection technique as scientific as possible.

(e) The size of the sample is also governed by the size of the tools to be used. In case the tools are short, and the questions asked pertain to certain limited factors, a large sample can be selected. In case the tools are large and the questions complicated, the sample should be small in size on that, from administrative point of view, the investigator may not be put to unnecessary troubles. In the present study, the tools were quite elaborate and large, hence a very large sample was not selected.

(f) The sampling method also determines the size of the sample. When random sampling method is used, the samples have to be large. On the other hand if samples are selected through stratified sampling method, the reliability can be achieved even with the help of the small-sized samples.

Taking into consideration all these factors which influence the size of the sample, it was decided that an ideal sample would consist of seven hundred students. This sample is small enough to avoid unnecessary expenditure and large enough to avoid intolerable sampling errors.

After deciding about the sampling method and the size of the sample, the universe selected was divided into different strata. The variables chosen for the study were considered to divide the universe. The variables chosen were—(1) residential versus non-residential schools (2) private versus government secondary schools (3) rural versus urban secondary schools (4) Telugu medium versus English medium secondary schools and (5) boys versus girls.

To select the sample, the Random Sampling Method was considered. In this method all the units from all types of secondary schools were given equal importance. The individual observations or individuals are chosen in such a way as each has an equal change of being selected, and that each choice is independent of any other choice. Random sampling may be done with the help of many methods. The lottery method suggested by Best was selected in this study.

After final selection the sample consisted of 700 secondary school students. The whole sample when divided consisted of residential 350 and non-residential 350, rural 350 and urban 350, private 400 and government 300, Telugu medium 400 and English medium 300, and boys 350 and girls 350.

The sampling design employed this involved not only the stratification of the universe but also random sampling technique to select samples from within the stratum.

SELECTION OF TOOLS

Research tools are the sole factors in determining the sound data and in drawing accurate conclusions about the problem on hand. The conclusions ultimately help in providing suitable remedial measures to the problem concerned.

The selection and use of tools can be done in two ways. The first one is to construct a tool independently by the researcher for his own study. Here, there are many problems in doing so. Preparation and standardization of a perfect tool itself is a major task, and one can say that it is a doctoral study itself. On construction of their own tools, Anand and Padma feel that a note on caution has to be struck when a researcher develops a tool for his study by merely pooling some items and does not subject it to the sophisticated techniques of tool construction. The result would be then obvious, a poor quality research.

The second way of selection and use of tools is right selection of tools from already standardized ones available in the field of study. Here also, it involves a tedious job in locating the tools and identifying their usefulness to the study on hand. Even then, this technique is very useful when a research work involves a good number of variables. Some people believe that some of the instruments available do not measure upto their standards. Hence, new ones. In some instances, consideration should be given to the logic of the situation. Lacking the time and financial resources of a test and measurement organization of researcher, many researchers cannot expect to produce a better instrument. In these cases, the most logical procedure that can follow is to choose the best instrument available for this purpose.

Considering the flaws and the merits of the selection of tools, the investigator is interested in using the standardized tools as the present study involves an intensive study of socio-economic status, educational aspirations and achievements in social studies of students studying in secondary schools.

MEASUREMENT OF SOCIO-ECONOMIC STATUS

After a thorough survey of literature, the investigator identified the following tools on socio-economic status which were found to be useful primarily. They include Kuppuswamy, Verma, Kulshresta, Shrivastava, Singh and Saxena, Udai Pareek and Trivedi, Rao, Patel, and Beena Shah. Among the tools available on SES prepared in Indian context, the SES developed Beena Shah was found most suitable for the present study as it contains all necessary aspects that contribute to the socio-economic status of an individual and as it was prepared more scientifically than any other taking into account the flaws of the SES scales.

The Socio-Economic Status scale thus selected was subjected to pretesting, which is, infact, a 'dress rehearsal' of the final study. The SES was administered to a sample of one hundred secondary school students. The reliability of SES was found 0.9. As this result was very close to the test result, this Socio-Economic Status scale of Beena Shah was finalized for the final administration to measure the socio-economic status of the sample. The particulars of the SES scale in detail are mentioned hereunder.

Socio-Economic Status Scale

The measurement of socio-economic status is a major operation in almost all researches related to social phenomenon. Basically, the whole concept of status has emerged in terms of social differentiation (Lintion 1936). Since, 1909, the efforts are being made to measure this phenomenon which being viewed now as the outcome of the interaction of various determinants. For example, Hollingshead (1949) considered occupation, education and residential address as determinants of socio-economic status (SES). Warner et.al. (1949) ignored education altogether and added income and type of housing to Hollingshead's categories Kahl (1957) added prestige, social-interaction, class-consciousness, value orientation and power to these categories and ignored education.

The measures developed by Kuppuswami (1962), Verma (1969), Kulshrestha (1972), Rao (1977), Srivastava (1978), Uniyal and Bisht (1982) and Rao (1982), etc. have incorporated variables like family size, education, occupation, social position, caste, land ownership, social participation and possessions.

The socio-economic scale was developed to identify the correct categories and minimize the perceptual content in SES and it was found that the socio-economic status can be measured more accurately with the help of the following variables—caste, occupation, education, income, possession, social participation.

The basic feature of this SES measure which is not in other tools of SES measurements is—

1. Occupational status is measured as the average score of two basic indicators of family occupation i.e., occupation of the parents (mother & father) and main occupation of the family.
2. Educational status of the family is considered with the help of educational level of father, mother and sibling (who has achieved the highest qualification among siblings). The average of the total scores obtained by these individual persons, is the measure of actual educational status of the family.
3. Economic status is measured not only with the help of father guardian's per month income, but in this SES scale total per month income of the family is divided by family size (total number of members of the family), to obtain the actual economic condition of the family. Two more questions related to income-tax and property-tax are also incorporated to this dimension in this SES scale. Weightage to different income categories is provided on the basis of standardized norms.
4. Weightage to different articles included in the list of possession has been assigned according to the cost and quality, that characterise their status.

Thus, this SES measure is made more improved and scientific. The details about the variables and their scoring procedure are given below.

Caste: Even today, in India, caste is found an important index of social status. In this SES scale the weightage to different caste groups is given, as—scheduled caste (1), scheduled tribes (2), backward castes (3), kayastha and other non-Hindu groups (4), vaishyas and kshatriyas (5) and brahmins (6).

Occupation: After conducting a survey of different occupations, this variable has been catergorized into five major categories on the continuum of occupational prestige. The weightage assigned to them varies from 1 to 12 e.g. category 5 (unskilled work etc.)—1 score, cateogry 4 killed work etc.,—2 scores, cateogry 3 clerk etc.,—4 scores, cateogry 2 non-gazetted officer etc. —8 scores and category 1 gazetted officer etc.—12 scores. The occupation of the father/guardian, mother and main occupation of the family are taken as the indicators of occupational/status. The occupational status score is the average of the scores of these two independent indicators. The weightage to the main occupation of the family has to be given in accordance with the above categories of the different occupations.

Education: The weightage assigned to all three indicators (father, mother and sibling), are the same for any given qualification, the eight categories of qualifications e.g., Illiterate (0), primary pass (1), high school pass (2), intermediate/ high school + some post high school diploma (3) B.A /B.Sc./ B.Com. B.Ed./ P.G., etc. (5) M.Ed./ M.B.B.S./ B.E. etc. (6) Ph.D./ M.S./ M.D./ M.E. etc. (7 scores), are arranged from illiterate to professional post-graduate degrees. The weightage assigned varies from 0 to 7. The educational status score is the average of the scores of the father, mother and sibling (only that member of siblings who has the achieved highest qualifications).

Income : Income is an index of economic status. Total monthly income of 630 students was recorded and after calculating the per capita income, it was converted into stanine scale. The IV and V and VI staines were grouped into one to form middle income groups. In the same way to form lower-middle and upper-middle income groups, II, III and VII and VIII staines were respectively grouped together. The I and IX staines were showing the low and high income groups respectively. The income groups and their respective weightages along with the stanines and percentages are given below.

DISTRIBUTION OF THE INCOME GROUPS

	Stanines				
	I	II III	IV V VI	VII VIII	IX
Percentage	0.91	14.96	68.34	14.96	0.91
Income-group	below 24	24 to 109	110 to 236	237 to 413	above 413
Weightage (Rs.)	1	2.5	5	7.5	9

Payment of income-tax and property-tax is also considered as the indicator of economic status. 1 score for 'Yes' and 9 scores for 'No' answer has to be given. Similarly for question No. 8. For a, b, c and d, answers 4, 3, 2 and 1, score is to given. Thus, the total of all these scores, is the economic condition of the family.

$$\text{Per capita income of the family} = \frac{\text{Total income of the family}}{\text{Total number of family members}}$$

Possession: Ownership of house—1 score for Yes and 0 score for No response. Type of house—for a Thatched house (1), Tiles house (2) and Building (3).

Number of rooms—one roomed house (1) two roomed house (2) three roomed house (3) four roomed house (4) and for five or more roomed house (5).

House—hold material—1 score for each of the following essentials of life: cooker, bicycle, radio, cooking-gas stove, water-pipe, electricity, electric fan, electric-press, furniture, alarm-clock.

2 score for each of the following essentials: tape-record, godrej almirah, carpet, wall-clock, dining-table, dinner-set, sewing-machine.

3 score for each item: calculator, type-writer, taperecorder cum transistor (2 in 1).

4 score for each single item: gun, pistol, record player.

5 score for each item: television, freeze, stereo, telephone, A.C., scooter, motor-cycle.

7 score for each item: jeep, car, tractor, truck.

Influx of newspapers and magazines—one score for one newspaper and one score for one magazine separately.

Animals—one score for one cow, an ox and one buffalo separately.

Land-ownership—one score for one bigha land; 2 scores for two bigha land, 3 scores for three bigha land and 4 scores for four bigha or more than four bigha land.

These are the six indicators of possession. Six questions are given on these variables and total scores are given on the basis of the quantity of the possessions.

Social Participation: To be a member of some association, to get award of honours, titles, etc., and involvement in social work, all these things affect the social status of a person. Four questions were given in the SES scale related to the above mentioned areas. One score was given for each positive response. Thus, minimum and maximum scores on this variables are 0 and 4 respectively.

The composit SES score is defined as the sum of the scores obtained on the above six variables i.e., caste, occupation, education, income, possession and social participation.

Development of Categories

The total possible categories were formed with the help of the scores on SES scale (obtained) after administering this scale among 630 students which were converted into stanine scale. The SES was classified into five categories i.e., lower status (LS), lower-middle status (LMS), middle status (MS), upper-middle status (UMS) and upper status (US). The MS was formed by adding the IV, V and VI stanines. Similarly, for LMS and UMS, II, III, VII and VIII Stanines were respectively combined together. LS and US were represented by I and IX stanines respectively. The percentages of the population contained in each class are given below in the Table.

STATUS CATEGORIES AND SCORES ON SES SCALE (N= 630)

	Stanines				
	I	II+III	IV + V + VI	VII + VIII	IX
Category	LS	LMS	MS	UMS	US
%	0.91	14.96	68.34	14.96	0.91
Scores	below 21	22-51	52-79	80-109	above 110

Reliability

The value of the reliability coefficients derived with the help of test-retest method, was found to be highly significant.

Reliability coefficients and Indexes of Reliability (test-retest method)

Time Interval	N	r	RI
20 days	225	0.92	0.96
30 days	225	0.89	0.94

Validity

To assess the validity of this SES scale, correlation coefficients of scores obtained on these 6 component variables with composite SES scores were calculated. The values are given.

Correlation Coefficients between total SES scores and scores on its component variables

Corre. Coef.	Caste	Occupa-tion	Educa-tion	Income	Posse-ssion	Social Partici-pation
r	0.72	0.82	0.86	0.83	0.78	0.69

The values of correlation coefficients (r) between composite SES scores and scores on individual six component variables were very high and statistically significant far beyond 0.001 level of significance. This indicates that the validity of this SES measure is of high order.

The composite scores of 630 students obtained on SES scale are distributed into 5 categories viz., LS, LMS, MS, UMS and US. The distribution of students in terms of frequency as well as percentages are shown below.

Distribution of students (N= 630) into different SES categories

	SES Categories				
	LS	LMS	MS	UMS	US
Observed (a) Frequencies	3	111	407	105	4
(b) Percentages	0.48	17.62	64.60	16.67	0.63
Theoretical (a) Frequencies	6	94	430	94	6
(b) Percentages	0.91	14.96	64.34	14.96	0.91

The study of above table reveals that the composite scores on SES scale of 630 students do not deviate significantly from the theoretical distribution (×2 = 7.75, n.s.). Hence, the distribution of the total SES scores is normal and its validity is of high order.

Since, the reliability and validity of this SES scale is of high order, it can be said with some amount of confidence that this measure will render an objective, effective and accurate assessment of one's socio-economic status whether belonging to urban or rural locality.

MEASUREMENT OF EDUCATIONAL ASPIRATIONS

To measure the educational aspirations of the senior intermediate students, an extensive survey was made to find out the suitable tool for this study. Through this survey, it was found that tools prepared on educational aspirations by Sexena, Sharma, and Gupta and Srivastava and Vansal are available for use in research studies. Out of these tools, it was identified that the educational aspirations tool prepared by Saxena was suitable for this study.

After identifying the suitability of the tool, the tool was administered to a sample of 100. The reliability of the tool in our conditions was found 0.87. As this result is nearer to the tool result, it was finalised to use in this study to measure the educational aspirations of secondary school students.

Educational Aspirations Scale

The fruitful approach to study the self-enhancement has been the concept of Aspiration Level. An individual's aspiration level represents him not only as he is at any particular moment, but also as he would like to be at some point in the future. It is a measure of his intentional disposition, an important element of his long range behaviour. By knowing a person's level of aspiration, we learn a great deal about him. So it is necessary to have some knowledge of the aspirational level of an individual, from both educational and guidance point of view.

The term, 'level of aspiration' is best defined by James Drever in his Dictionary of Psychology as a frame of reference involving self-esteem or alternatively as a standard with reference to which an individual experiences, i.e., has the feeling of failure or success. According to Bhargava, V.P. (1975), there are four typical sequence of events in a level of aspiration situation. The graphical representation of these sequence of events is given below:

1	2	3	4
Last Performance	Setting of level of Aspiration	New Performance	Time Reaction to New Performance
Goal Discrepancy (Difference between 2-1)		Attainment Discrepancy	
(Difference between 3-2) (New Performance minus goal set)		Feeling of Success or Failure related to differences of Levels 3 and 2	

Explaining the time sequence Bhargava further adds that difference between level of last performance and the level of new goal (2-1) is called goal discrepancy and the difference between the goal level and that of new performance (3-2) is called attainment discrepancy. This difference is the basis of the reaction at point 4.

The concept of level of aspiration was first introduced by Hoppe (1930) while making a reference to the 'degree of difficulty of the goal towards which a person is striving', and the first presentation of the theoretical concept of level of aspiration was made by Escalona which was further elaborated by Festinger in 1942, Dembo and Sears in 1944. Other pioneer works in this area include those of Pareek (1958), Sinha, D.N. (1969), Bhargava, V.P. (1975), Tiwari, G. and Sigh, H.M. (1976), etc.

Unemployment, underemployment and unsuitable employment are some of the major problems we are faced with at present in our country. Educational institutions are charged with the responsibility of developing vocational behaviours which may solve some of these problems. In other words, the system of education must meet the requirements of the society. In order that useful vocational behaviours may be developed among the adolescents, initial choice and later adjustment to courses and careers depends largely on the wisdom shown at the initial choice stages. Right type of curricular choices and vocational decisions therefore have come to occupy a central place in the lives of adolescents. It is as much essential as to know the nature of educational aspirations of an individual. The present scale is a humble attempt in this direction, though several attempts have been made by psychologists from time to time as Hatt (1950), Empy (1956) , Sewell, Haller and Strauss (1957), Stern (1958), Pace (1963), Rosenberg (1965), Grewal (1975), Tiwari and Singh (1976) and several others but still there is paucity in the measuring of educational aspirations of an individual. The present scale attempts to fill in this lacuna. Level of educational aspiration here has been considered as a concept, referring to orientation towards educational goal, spaced in continuum of difficulty and social prestige and arranged in educational hierarchy.

Construction and Standardization

The present scale is developed on the concept and technique of Haller and Miller (1963) under Indian conditions. This educational aspiration scale has been designed on the strength of the lists of degrees, diplomas, certificates and other distinctive educational qualifications as maintained by different Indian Universities, Competitive Examination Boards in India and a list of 150 educational status of different levels was collected. The items of qualifications were reviewed carefully and 50 items were detected by 10 judges of college faculty on the basis of duplication and inadequacy. This list was given to a 100 individuals asking them to rate on a five-point scale ranging from excellent to poor standing. Social standing of each qualification was calculated out of the rank of 100 by multiplying frequency ratings in each of the five categories by 1.0, 0.8, 0.6, 0.4, 0.2 respectively. Thus ranked from 0 to 9 depending upon the ranks and ranged from 20 to 95 and above were taken for consideration and 80 qualifications with different prestige values were arranged in mixed order in 10 multiple choice items in the form as given below in the final form of the scale.

	Goal Periods	
Expression Levels	Short Range	Long Range
Idealistic	Of the jobs listed below which one would you choose if you were free to choose any one of them you wished when your education is over? 3, 8	Of the jobs listed below which one would you choose to to have when you are 25 years old if you were free to have any one of them you wished? 2, 7
Realistic	Of the jobs listed below which is the best one you are really sure you can get when your education is over? 1, 5	Of the jobs listed below which is the best one you are really sure you can get by the time you become 25 years old? 4, 6

The qualification for each item was used only once in the scale. The final form of the scale was administered to a group of 200 students of college level including males and females selected randomly from Hindi as well English medium. The correlation coefficient between the two groups (English medium and Hindi medium students) was found to be 0.82 which shows that both the versions of the present scale have appropriate value of understanding the content.

Administration

The present scale is self administering which can be administered individually or in a group. There is no time limit but usually its completion takes 15 to 20 minutes. The test is required to fill the general information and read the instructions carefully given on the first page, before starting the work.

Reliability

The scale was measured for its Test-retest reliability by administering to a group of 200 college students including boys and girls aged 17 years with an interval of one month and the reliability coefficient was found to be 0.86 and the interval consistency between the two halves (i.e., realistic and idealistic) was found to be 0.698.

Validity

As pointed out earlier the items of the present scale were collected either or from the available literature from the existing standardized tools in this field which indirectly show that the scale has internal validity. To know the external validity, the present scale, when along with Sharma and Gupta's Educational Aspiration Scale administered to a 100 college students with an interval of one week. Os. 81 coefficient of validity was found and when it was administered along with Tiwari and Singh's Level of Aspiration Scale, the validity coefficient was calculated to be 0.86 and when administered along with Haller and Miller's Aspiration Scale, 0.84 validity coefficient was found.

Scoring Procedure

Very simple procedure has been adopted for the purpose of scoring. Score have been given to each qualification on the basis of prestige value. While scoring it should be kept in mind that only one alternative should be checked from each category. The scores for the 10 alternatives should be given in the following manner:

Alternatives	Scores
1.1	9
1.2	6
1.3	8
1.4	2
1.5	7
1.6	0
1.7	5
1.8	3
1.9	1
1.10	4

Interpretation of Scores

Norms have been developed for the interpretation of the scores. For this purpose 2000 samples were taken from both sexes, males and females of B.A., B.Sc., and B.Com., level of rural and urban area from middle social class family of Kanpur region. At the first stage the marks of intermediate exams were obtained and only those students who achieved either more than 55 per cent marks (high achievers) and below 40 per cent marks (low achievers) were selected. Thus only 860 (430 high achievers and 430 low achievers) were selected from the 2000 subjects for calculating H.A. and L.A. norms. The total norms were obtained from the sample of 2000 students. The present test was administered to 860 subjects and percentile norms were calculated separately for boys and girls, and high and low achievers. The percentile norms are given in the following table:

Percentile	Boys		Girls		Total
	H.A. N= 240	L.A. N=190	H.A. N—210	L.A. N—220	N=860
P 99	65	50	64	45	63
P 98	64	49	60	40	60
P 95	63	45	59	36	57
P 90	62	44	57	35	51
P 80	57	40	56	34	46
P 75	54	38	54	31	43
P 60	52	36	51	28	37
P 50	48	33	48	27	35
P 40	46	30	45	25	32
P 30	44	28	40	23	30
P 25	38	24	39	20	27
P 10	26	21	28	19	22
P 5	23	18	25	17	19
P 1	19	16	20	14	16

In the present study, a student can get a maximum score of 72 and a minimum score of 0.

MEASUREMENT OF ACHIEVEMENT

To measure the achievement in social studies of each student, the marks of quarterly, half-yearly, pre-public examinations conducted throughout the academic year were added and converted into averages. Each student has got an average score of his whole year's academic performance in social studies and it was used as the score of achievement in social studies.

4

ANALYSIS OF DATA

The organization, analysis and interpretation of data and formulation of conclusions are necessary steps to get a meaningful picture out of the raw information collected. The analysis and interpretation of data involve the objective material in the possession of the researcher and his subjective reactions and desires to derive from the data the inherent meanings in their relation to the problem (Rummel, 1958).

The mass data collected through the use of various tools, need to be systematized and organized, i.e., edited, classified and tabulated before it can serve the purpose. Hence, editing implies the checking of gathered data for accuracy, utility and completeness; classifying refers to the dividing of the information into recording of the classified material in accurate mathematical terms. Analysis of data means studying the tabulated material in order to determine inherent facts or meanings. It involves breaking down the existing complex factors into simple parts and putting the parts together in new arrangements for the purpose of interpretation.

After the data collection was finished, it was analysed keeping in view the objectives and hypotheses of the study. The present study includes five major aspects, viz., socio-economic status, educati—onal aspirations, achievement in social studies, the relationship between socio-economic status and achievement in social studies and educational aspirations and achievement in social studies. Through the tools used, the total scores of socio-economic status scale and educational aspirations scale were taken as raw scores for analysis and the average marks of each student in their quarterly, half-yearly, pre-public, public examination in Social studies were also collected from the respective secondary schools.

The score of socio-economic status scale, educational aspirations scale and average marks of each student were used as basic sources of data for the study. These scores were put to statistical treatment. The hypotheses framed were statistically tested and accordingly accepted or rejected. The data were thus statistically treated and the results are presented in the following pages.

SOCIO-ECONOMIC STATUS

The score of socio-economic status scale was taken to find out the socio-economic status (SES) of the secondary school students. On the advice of experts, the socio-economic status was divided into three categories, viz., low status, middle status and upper status for statistical convenience and easy identification. The student who scored below 21 was put in low status group, the student who scored between 22 and 109 was put in middle status group and the student who scored 110 and above was put in high status group.

The mean score was used to identify the socio-economic status of total secondary school students and to compare the sub-sample variation. The values of standard deviation were used to measure the spread or dispersion of scores in the distribution. The critical ratios were calculated to test the significant difference in the means of the two sub-samples of each variable. The chi-square test of independence was applied for comparing the experimentally obtained results with those to be expected theoretically on the hypotheses.

Hypothesis 1 : The Secondary School Students do not possess high socio-economic status.

To test the validity of Hypothesis 1, the total scores of socio-economic status scale of the whole sample were calculated to arrive at the mean and standard deviation. The results are as follows:

Table 4.1 : SES of the whole sample

Sample	Sample size	Mean	Standard Deviation
Whole	700	61.89	33.66

From Table 4.1, it is clear that the Secondary School students had middle socio-economic status. As per the standard deviation value, the dispersion of SES was high in the units of the sample.

The chi-square test of independence was applied to test the divergence of observed results from those expected theoretically.

Table 4. 2 : Distribution of SES in whole sample

Sample size		Low status [LS]	Middle status [MS]	High status [HS]	Chi-square (X^2)
700	fo	283	358	59	315.41 *
	fe	112	476	112	

* Significant at 0.01 level.
fo–frequency of occurrence of observed facts
fe–frequency of occurrence expected theoretically
P–at 0.01 level is 9, 21
df = 2

As the chi-square test value was significant, the SES of Secondary School students was not distributed normally. The SES trend towards low SES.

So, the hypothesis that "the Secondary School students do not possess high socio-economic status" can be accepted.

Hypothesis 1 A : There is no significant difference in the level of Socio-Economic Status of residential and non-residential Secondary School Students.

To compare the difference in the level of SES of residential and non-residential Secondary School students, the following statistical treatment was given.

Table 4.3 : Comparison of SES of Residential and Non-Residential students

Variable	Sample size	Mean	S.D.	M.D.	S.E.D.	Critical Ratio
Residential	350	64.29	32.66	4.8	2.53	1.89 +
Non-residential	350	59.49	34.46			

+ Not significant at 0.01 level.

As per Table 4.3, there was no significant difference in the SES of residential and non-residential secondary school students.

Though there was no significant difference in the level of SES, the distribution of it was studied in both the sub-samples.

Table 4.4 : Distribution of SES in Residential and Non-Residential students

Variable	Sample size		Low status	Middle status	High status	Chi-square
Residential	350	fo	134	187	29	132.57*
		fe	56	238	56	
Non-Residential	350	fo	149	171	30	185.37*
		fe	56	238	56	

* Significant at 0.01 level.

The distribution of SES was not normal in both the cases. In both the samples, the middle SES students were more.

The hypothesis that 'there is no significant difference in the level of Socio-Economic Status of residential and non-residential Secondary School students' can be accepted.

Hypothesis 1 B : There is no significant difference in the level of Socio-Economic Status of rural and urban Secondary School students.

A comparison was made to identify the difference in the level of SES of students studying in rural and urban secondary schools. The results are as follows :

Table 4.5 : Comparison of SES of Rural and Urban Students

Variable	Sample size	Mean	S.D.	M.D.	S.E.D.	Critical Ratio
Rural	350	61.2	32.91	1.37	2.54	0.54+
Urban	350	62.57	34.37			

+ Not significant at 0.01 level.

There is no significant difference in the level of SES in rural and urban secondary school students.

Though there was no significant difference in the level of SES between rural and urban students, its distribution was studied in both cases.

Table 4.6 : Distribution of SES in Rural and Urban Students

Variable	Sample size	Low status	Middle status	High status	Chi-square
Rural 350	fo	126	196	28	108.91 *
	fe	56	238	56	
Urban 350	fo	144	171	35	165.01 *
	fe	56	238	56	

* Significant at 0.01 level.

The distribution of SES in both the cases was not normal. The middle status students were more followed by low status in both the cases.

So, the hypothesis that 'there is no significant difference in the level of Socio-Economic Status of Rural and Urban Secondary School Students' can be accepted.

Hypothesis 1 C: There is no significant difference in the level of Socio-Economic Status of Private and Government Secondary School Students.

To identify the difference between private and government school students, the following statistical treatment was given and the results are as follows :

Table 4.7 : Comparison of SES of Private and Government School Students

Variable	Sample size	Mean	S.D.	M.D.	S.E.D.	Critical Ratio
Private	400	68.7	24.38	15.9	2.18	7.29
Government	300	52.8	31.49			

* Significant at 0.01 level.

There was a significant difference in the level of SES between the students studying in private schools and government schools. The students studying in private schools possessed more SES to their counterparts.

As there is a difference in the SES of students studying in private schools and government schools, the distribution of it was studied in both the cases.

Table 4.8 : Distribution of SES in Private and Government School Students

Variable	Sample size	Low status	Middle status	High status	Chi-square
Private 400	fo	126	231	43	73.13*
	fe	64	272	64	
Government 300	fo	157	127	16	297.91*
	fe	48	204	48	

* Significant at 0.01 level.

The distribution of SES was not normal in both the cases. More than half of the students were in middle SES in case of students studying in private school and the same was there in low SES in case of students studying in government schools.

Hence, the hypothesis that 'there is no significant difference in the level of Socio-Economic Status of Private and Government Secondary School Students' can be rejected.

Hypothesis 1 D: There is no significant difference in the level of Socio-Economic Status of Telugu medium and English medium Secondary School students.

A comparison was made to identify the difference in the level of SES of students studying in Telugu medium and English medium secondary schools. The results are as follows:

Table 4.9 : Comparison of SES of Telugu Medium and English Medium Students

Variable	Sample size	Mean	S.D.	M.D.	S.E.D.	Critical Ratio
Telugu medium	400	51.75	30.65	23.65	2.43	0.73 *
English medium	300	75.4	32.72			

Significant at 0.01 level.

As per the values of mean and critical ratio, the students studying in english Medium schools possessed more SES than their counterparts.

As there was a significant difference in the level of SES of Telugu medium and English medium students, it was tried to identify the distribution of SES in both the cases.

Table 4.10 : Distribution of SES in Telugu Medium and English Medium Students;

Variable	Sample size		Low status	Middle status	High status	Chi-square
Telugu medium	400	fo	213	169	18	418.95*
		fe	64	272	64	
English medium	300	fo	72	187	41	14.43 *
		fe	48	204	48	

* Significant at 0.01 level.

As per the values of Table 4.10, more than half of them were in low SES in case of Telugu medium students and in middle SES in case of English medium students.

Hence, the hypothesis that 'there is no significant difference in the level of Socio-Economic Status of Telugu medium and English medium Secondary School Students' can be rejected.

Hypothesis 1 E: There is no significant difference in the level of Socio-Economic Status of Boys and Girls.

A comparison was made to identify the difference in the level of SES of boys and girls studying in Secondary Schools.

Table 4.11 : Comparison of Boys and Girls

Variable	Sample	Mean	S.D.	M.D.	S.E.D.	Critical Ratio
Boys	350	57.94	33.49	7.89	2.52	3.13 +
Girls	350	65.83	33.35			

+ Not significant at 0.01 level.

According to the mean values and critical ratio, there was no significant difference in the SES of boys and girls.

Though there was no significant difference in the level of SES of boys and girls it was tried to identify the distribution of SES in both the cases.

Table 4.12: Distribution of SES in Boys and Girls

Variable	Sample size	Low status	Middle status	High status	Chi-square
Boys 350	fo	169	159	25	273.42 *
	fe	56	238	56	
Girls 350	fo	114	202	34	74.15 *
	fe	56	238	56	

* Significant at 0.01 level.

As per the above results there are more girls in average SES and SES trend is moving towards low SES in boys.

So, the hypothesis that 'there is no significant difference in the level of Socio-Economic Status of boys and girls' can be accepted.

EDUCATIONAL ASPIRATIONS

The scores of educational aspirations scale were taken into consideration to find out the educational aspirations of secondary school students. The maximum score a student can get was 72. A student who secured 24 and below was put in low aspiration group, a student who secured in between 25 and 48 was put in average aspiration group, and a student who secured 49 and above was put in high aspiration group.

The mean scores were used to identify the educational aspirations of the Secondary School students. The values of standard deviation were used to measure the dispersion of scores in the distribution of educational aspirations in the students. The critical ratios were calculated to test the significant difference in the means of the sub samples of each variable. The chi-square test of independence was applied for comparing the experimentally obtained results with those to be expected theoretically on the hypotheses.

Hypothesis 2 : The Secondary School students do not possess high Educational aspirations.

To test the validity of Hypothesis 2, the total scores of the whole sample were calculated to arrive at mean and standard deviation, results obtained are as follows:

Table 4.13 : Educational Aspirations of the whole sample

Sample	Sample size	Mean	Standard Deviation
Whole	700	38.27	13.96

It is clear, from the above table, that the secondary school students possessed an average level of educational aspirations. The score, as per standard deviation, dispersed to a reasonable extent in the sample.

To test the divergence of observed facts from those expected theoretically, the chi-square test of independence was applied. The results are given here under:

Table 4.14 : Distribution of Educational Aspirations in the Whole Sample

Sample size	Low	Average	High	Chi-square
700 fo	77	490	133	15.27*
fe	112	476	112	

* Significant at 0.01 level.

As per the significant value of chi-square, the educational aspirations of Secondary School students were not normally distributed. More than two thirds of students are possessed average educational aspirations followed by nearly one-fourth of students who possessed high educational aspirations.

So, the hypothesis that 'the Secondary School Students do not possess high educational aspirations' can be accepted.

Hypothesis 2 A : There is no significant difference in the level of educational aspirations of residential and non-residential secondary school students.

To compare the difference in the level of educational aspirations possessed by residential and non-residential school students, the following statistical treatment was given:

Table 4.15 : Comparison of Educational Aspirations of Residential and Non-Residential students

Variable size	Sample	Mean	S.D.	M.D.	S.E.D.	Critical Ratio
Residential	350	39.86	13.57	3.17	1.05	3.02 *
Non-residential	350	36.69	14.17			

* Significant at 0.01 level.

There was a marginally significant difference in the level of educational aspirations possessed by the residential and non-residential students. The residential students aspired a little bit higher to their counterparts.

As there was difference in the level of educational aspirations of residential and non-residential students, it was tried to identify the distribution of educational aspirations in the sub-samples.

Table 4.16 : Distribution of Educational Aspirations in Residential and Non-Residential Students

Variable	Sample size	Low	Average	High	Chi-square
Residential 350	fo	29	242	79	22.51*
	fe	56	238	56	
Non-residential 350	fo	49	247	54	1.28+
	fe	56	238	56	

* Significant at 0.01 level.
\+ Not significant at 0.01 level.

As per Table 4.16, the distribution of educational aspirations were not distributed normally in residential students and distributed normally in non-residential students. The trend of educational aspirations moved towards high in residential school students.

Hence, the hypothesis that 'there is no significant difference in the level of educational aspirations of residential and non-residential secondary school students' can be rejected.

Hypothesis 2 B: There is no significant difference in the level of educational aspirations of rural and urban secondary school students.

Table 4.17 : Comparison of Educational Aspirations of Rural and Urban students

Variable	Sample size	Mean	S.D.	M.D.	S.E.D.	Critical Ratio
Rural	350	38.57	14.24	0.6	1.05	0.57+
Urban	350	37.97	13.65			

+ Not significant at 0.01 level.

As per the values of the mean and critical ratio, there was no significant difference in the level of educational aspirations possessed by the rural and urban school students.

Though there was no significant difference in the level of educational aspirations of rural and urban students, it was tried to identify the distribution of educational aspirations in the sub-samples.

Table 4.18 : Distribution of Educational Aspirations of Rural and Urban Students

Variable	Sample size	Low	Average	High	Chisquare
Rural 350	fo	51	235	64	1.61+
	fe	56	238	56	
Urban 350	fo	40	245	65	6.21+
	fe	56	238	56	

+ Not significant at 0.01 level.

The distribution of educational aspirations, as per the Table 4.18, was distributed normally in both the cases.

So, the hypothesis that 'there is no significant difference in the level of educational aspirations of rural and urban secondary school students can be accepted.

Hypothesis 2 C: There is no significant difference in the level of educational aspirations of Private and Government Secondary School students.

To identify the difference in the level of educational aspirations possessed by private and government school students, the following statistical treatment was given.

Table 4.19 : Comparison of Educational Aspirations of Private and Government School students

Variable	Sample size	Mean	S.D.	M.D.	S.E.D.	Critical Ratio
Private	400	39	14.07	17	1.06	1.6+
Government	300	37.3	13.77			

+ Not significant at 0.01 level.

There was no significant difference in the level of educational aspirations possessed by the students studying in private and government secondary schools.

Though there was no significant difference in the level of educational aspirations possessed by the private and government school students, it was tried to identify the distribution of educational aspirations in both the cases.

Table 4.20 : Distribution of Educational Aspirations in Private and Government School Students

Variable	Sample size	low	Average	High	Chi-square
Private 400	fo	39	273	88	18.76*
	fe	64	272	64	
Government 300	fo	39	216	45	2.57+
	fe	48	204	48	

* Significant at 0.01 level.
+ Not significant at 0.01 level.

As per the chi-square values, the educational aspirations were distributed not normally in private school students and distributed normally in the government school students. A marginal high number of students studying in private schools possessed high educational aspirations.

So, the hypothesis that 'there is no significant difference in the level of educational aspirations of private and government secondary school students' can be accepted.

Hypothesis 2 D : There is no significant difference in the level of educational aspirations of Telugu medium and English medium Secondary School students.

A comparison was made to identify the difference in the level of educational aspirations possessed by the students studying in Telugu medium and English medium secondary schools.

Table 4.21 : Comparison of Educational Aspirations of Telugu Medium and English Medium Students

Variable	Sample size	Mean	S.D.	M.D.	S.E.D.	Critical Ratio
Telugu medium	400	37.27	14.10	2.33	1.05	2.21*
English medium	300	39.6	13.66			

* Significant at 0.01 level.

There was a significant difference in the level of educational aspirations possessed by the students studying in Telugu medium and English medium. The English medium students possessed slightly high educational aspirations than their counterparts.

As there was a significant difference in the educational aspirations possessed by the Telugu medium and English medium students, it was studied to identify the distribution of educational aspirations in the variables.

Table 4.22 : Distribution of Educational Aspirations in Telugu Medium and English Medium Students.

Variable	Sample size		Low	Average	High	Chi-square
Telugu medium	400	fo	51	288	61	3.72+
		fe	64	272	64	
English medium	300	fo	27	201	72	21.23*
		fe	48	204	48	

+ Not significant at 0.01 level.
* Significant at 0.01 level.

The educational aspirations were distributed normally in Telugu medium students and distributed not normally in English medium students. The trend of educational aspirations moving, towards high in case of English medium students.

Hence, the hypothesis that 'there is no significant difference in the level of educational aspirations of Telugu medium and English medium secondary school students' can be rejected.

Hypothesis 2 E : There is no significant difference in the level of educational aspirations of boys and girls.

A comparison was made to study the difference in the level of educational aspirations possessed by boys and girls.

Table 4.23 : Comparison of Educational Aspirations of Boys and Girls

Variable	Sample size	Mean	S.D.	M.D.	S.E.D.	Critical Ratio
Boys	350	40.03	13.26	3.52	1.04	3.38*
Girls	350	36.51	14.43			

* Significant at 0.01 level.

There was a significant difference in the level of educational aspirations possessed by boys and girls. Boys possessed slightly higher educational aspirations than girls.

As there was a significant difference in the level of educational aspirations possessed by boys and girls, it was tried to study the distribution of educational aspirations in the variables.

Table 4.24 : Distribution of Educational Aspirations in Boys and Girls

Variable	Sample size	Low	Average	High	Chi-square
Boys 350	fo	30	247	73	17.57 *
	fe	56	238	56	
Girls 350	fo	48	242	60	1.49+
	fe	56	238	56	

* significant at 0.01 level.
\+ Not significant at 0.01 level.

The distribution of educational aspirations was normal in girls and not normal in boys. The trend of educational aspirations moved towards high in boys.

So, the hypothesis that 'there is no significant difference in the level of educational aspirations of boys and girls' can be rejected.

ACHIEVEMENT IN SOCIAL STUDIES

To measure the achievement in social studies of each student, the marks of quarterly, half-yearly, pre-public and public examinations conducted throughout the academic year were added and converted them into averages. Each student will get an average score and it will be his achievement in that academic year.

In Andhra Pradesh a student who secured 39 per cent and less than it will be put in third class, a student who secured in between 40-49 per cent will be put in second class and a student who secured 60 per cent and above will be put in first class. By following this classification in this study also, a student who secured 39 and less was put in low achievement group, a student who secured in between 40 and 59 was put in average achievement group, and a student who secured 60 and above was put in high achievement group.

The mean scores were used to identify the achievement of the sample. The values of standard deviation were used to measure the dispersion of scores in the distribution. The critical ratios were calculated to test the significant difference in the means of the two sub-samples of each variable. The chi-square test of independence was applied for comparing the experimentally obtained results with those to be expected theoretically on the hypothesis.

Hypothesis 3 : The Secondary school students do not possess high achievement in social studies.

To test the validity of the above hypotheses, the achievement scores of the whole sample were put to Statistical treatment to arrive at results.

Table 4.25 : Achievement in Social Studies of the Whole Sample.

Sample	Sample size	Mean	Standard Deviation
Whole	700	63.85	19.41

The secondary school students were with high achievement. The dispersion of the scores in the whole sample was also to reasonable extend.

The chi-square test of independence was applied to test the divergence of observed results from those expected theoretically.

Table 4.26 : Distribution of Achievement in Social Studies in Whole Sample.

Sample size		Low	Average	High	Chi-square
700	fo	24	238	438	1136.14*
	fe	112	476	112	

* Significant at 0.01 level.

As per the above very high significant value of the chi-square, the achievement in social studies was not normally distributed. The achievement trend inclined very much towards high achievement.

So, the hypothesis that 'the Secondary School Students do not possess high achievement in Social Studies' can be rejected.

Hypothesis 3 A : There is no significant difference in the level of achievement in Social Studies of Residential and Non-Residential Secondary School students.

Table 4.27 : Comparison of Achievement in Social Studies of Residential and Non-Residential Students

Variable	Sample size	Mean	S.D.	M.D.	S.E.D.	Critical Ratio
Residential	350	67.1	18.62	6.5	1.44	4.5*
Non-Residential	350	60.6	19.64			

* Significant at 0.01 level.

There was a significant difference in the level of achievement of Residential and Non-Residential students. The residential students were superior than their counterparts in the achievement in Social Studies, though both of them held high achievement.

As there was a significant difference in the level of achievement of residential and non-residential students, it was tried to study the distribution of achievement in both the cases.

Table 4.28 : Distribution of Achievement in Social Studies in Residential and Non Residential Students

Variable	Sample size	Low	Average	High	Chi-square
Residential 350	fo	3	91	256	855.23*
	fe	56	238	56	
Non-residential 350	fo	21	147	182	340.16*
	fe	56	238	56	

* Significant at 0.01 level.

The distribution of achievement in Social Studies was not normal in both the cases. The achievement concentration in both the cases was in high category, but this was very high in residential students.

Hence, the hypothesis that 'there is no significant difference in the level of achievement in Social Studies of residential and non-residential secondary school students' can be rejected.

Hypothesis 3 B: There is no significant difference in the level of achievement in Social Studies of rural and urban secondary school students.

To compare the achievement in Social Studies of rural and urban secondary school students, the following calculation were carried out.

Table 4.29: Comparison of Achievement in Social Studies of Rural and Urban Students.

Variable	Sample size	Mean	S.D.	M.D.	S.E.D.	Critical Ratio
Rural	350	61.9	18.77	3.9	1.45	2.68*
Urban	350	65.8	19.83			

* Significant at 0.01 level.

As per the mean values, the urban students possessed slightly high achievement in Social Studies, though both of them were with high achievement.

As there was a significant difference in the level of achievement of rural and urban students, it was studied to identity the distribution of achievement in both the sub-samples.

Table 4.30 : Distribution of Achievement in Social Studies in Rural and Urban Students

Variable	Sample size	Low	Average	High	Chi-square
Rural 350	fo	11	129	210	626.05*
	fe	56	238	56	
Urban 350	fo	13	109	228	631.21*
	fe	56	238	56	

* Significant at 0.01 level.

The achievement trend in both the cases inclined towards high achievement category and more than half of the students were in high achievement group.

So, the hypothesis that ' there is no significant difference in the level of achievement in Social Studies of rural and urban secondary school students' can be rejected.

Hypothesis 3 C : There is no significant difference in the level of achievement in Social Studies of private and government secondary school students.

A comparison was made between achievement levels of private and government school students.

Table 4.31 : Comparison of Achievement in Social Studies in Private and Government School Students

Variable	Sample size	Mean	S.D.	M.D.	S.E.D.	Critical Ratio
Private	400	62.73	18.08	0.15	1.52	0.09+
Government	300	62.88	21.25			

+ Not significant at 0.01 level.

There was no significant difference in the level of achievement in Social Studies of private and government secondary school students, though both the cases were with high achievement.

Though there was no significant difference in the level of achievement of private and government school students, it was studied the distribution of achievement in both the cases.

Table 4.32: Distribution of Achievement in Social Studies in Private and Government School students.

Variable	Sample size	Low	Average	High	Chi-square
Private 400	fo	3	125	272	813.58*
	fe	64	272	64	
Government 300	fo	21	113	166	345.86*
	fe	48	204	48	

* Significant at 0.01 level.

The achievement in both the cases was not normally distributed. The achievement trend in both the cases inclined towards high achievement category. In private schools, nearly one-third of the students were in high achievement group.

Hence, the hypothesis that ' there is no significant difference in the level of achievement in Social Studies of private and government secondary school students' can be accepted.

Hypothesis 3 D : There is no significant difference in the level of achievement in Social Studies of Telugu medium and English medium Secondary School students.

A comparison was made between the achievement levels of Telugu medium and English medium students.

Table 4.33 : Comparison of Achievement in Social Studies of Telugu medium and English medium students

Variable	Sample size	Mean	S.D.	M.D.	S.E.D.	Critical Ratio
Telugu medium	400	61.95	20.32	6.41	1.44	4.45*
English medium	300	68.36	17.88			

* Significant at 0.01 level.

There was a significant difference in the level of achievement of Telugu medium and English medium students, though both the cases possessed high achievement.

As there was a significant difference in level of achievement of Telugu medium and English medium students, the distribution of achievement in both the cases was studied.

Table 4.34 : Distribution of Achievement in Social Studies in Telugu medium and English medium students.

Variable	Sample size		Low	Average	High	Chi-square
Telugu medium	400	fo	23	157	220	455.13*
		fe	64	272	64	
English medium	300	fo	1	81	218	722.26*
		fe	48	204	48	

* Significant at 0.01 level.

The distribution of achievement in both cases was not normally distributed and the achievement trend inclined towards high achievement group. More than one-third of the English medium students were in high achievement category and more than half of the Telugu medium students were in high achievement category.

Consequently, the hypothesis that 'there is no significant difference in the level of achievement in Social Studies of Telugu medium and English medium Secondary School students' can be accepted.

Hypothesis 3 E : There is no significant difference in the level of achievement in Social Studies of boys and girls.

A comparison was made between the achievement of boys and girls to identify the difference between them.

Table 4.35 : Comparison of achievement in Social Studies of Boys and Girls

Variable	Sample size	Mean	S.D.	M.D.	S.E.D.	Critical Ratio
Boys	350	65.4	18.65	3.1	1.46	2.12*
Girls	350	62.3	20.02			

* Significant at 0.01 level.

There was a significant difference in the achievement of boys and girls. Boys were possessing a little bit high achievement than girls, though both of them possessed high achievement.

As there was a significant difference in the level of achievement of boys ànd girls, the distribution of it was studied in both the cases.

Table 4.36 : Distribution of Achievement in Social Studies in Boys and Girls

Variable	Sample size	Low	Average	High	Chi-square
Boys 350	fo	6	103	241	732.37*
	fe	56	238	56	
Girls 350	fo	18	135	197	425.36*
	fe	56	238	56	

*Significant at 0.01 level.

In both the cases, the distribution of achievement was not normal and the achievement inclined towards high achievement category. More than two-third of boys and half of the girls were in high achievement category.

So, the hypothesis that 'there is no significant difference in the level of achievement in Social Studies of boys and girls' can be rejected.

Relationship Between Socio-Economic Status And Achievement in Social Studies

The present study also aims at identifying the relationship between socio-economic status and achievement in social studies. To identify the relationship between these two, the chi-square of independence was applied. The results are as follows:

Hypothesis 4 : There is no significant association between socio-economic status and achievement in Social Studies in Secondary School students.

To test the validity of the above hypothesis, the chi-square value was computed for the whole sample.

Table 4.37 : Association between Socio-Economic Status and Achievement in Social Studies

Sample	Sample size	Chi-square
Whole	700	5.76+

+ Not significant at 0.01 level.

As per the chi-square value, there was no relationship between socio-economic status and achievement in Social Studies.

Hence, the hypothesis that ' there is no significant association between socio-economic status and achievement in Social Studies in Secondary School students' can be accepted.

Hypothesis 4 A : There is no significant association between Socio-economic status and achievement in Social Studies in Residential and Non-Residential Secondary School students.

The chi-square values were calculated to identify the validity of the above hypothesis.

Table 4.38 : Association between SES and Achievement in Residential and Non-Residential Students

Variable	Sample size	Chi-square
Residential	350	3.99+
Non-Residential	350	9.25*

+ Not significant at 0.01 level.
* Significant at 0.01 level.

There was no significant association between socio-economic status and achievement in Social Studies in case of residential students, but there was a positive association between socio-economic status and achievement in case of non-residential students.

The hypothesis that 'there is no association between socio-economic status and achievement in Social Studies in residential and non-residential students' can be partially rejected and partially accepted.

Hypothesis 4 B : There is no significant association between Socio-Economic Status and achievement in Social Studies in Rural and Urban Secondary School students.

To test the validity of the above hypothesis, the chi-square values were calculated.

Table 4.39 : Association between SES and Achievement in Rural and Urban Students.

Variable	Sample size	Chi-square
Rural	350	0.67+
Urban	350	3.66+

+ Not significant at 0.01 level.

There was no significant relationship between socio-economic status and achievement in both the cases.

Hence, the hypothesis that 'there is no significant association between socio-economic status and achievement in Social Studies in rural and urban Secondary School students' can be accepted.

Hypothesis 4 C : There is no significant association between socio-economic status and Achievement in Social Studies in Private and Government Secondary School students.

Chi-square values were calculated to test the validity of the above hypothesis.

Table 4.40 : Association between SES and achievement in Private and Government School students

Variable	Sample size	Chi-square
Private	400	6.92+
Government	300	2.91+

+ Not significant at 0.01 level.

There was no significant association between socio-economic status and achievement in social studies in both the cases.

So, the hypothesis that 'there is no significant association between socio-economic status and achievement in Social Studies in private and government secondary school students' can be accepted.

Hypothesis 4 D : There is no significant association between socio-Economic Status and Achievement in Social Studies in Telugu medium and English medium Secondary School students.

To test the validity of the above hypothesis, the chi-square values were calculated.

Table 4.41 : Association between SES and Achievement in Telugu medium and English medium students

Variable	Sample size	Chi-Square
Telugu medium	400	2.66+
English medium	300	3.81 +

+ Not significant at 0.01 level.

There was no significant relationship between Socio-Economic status and achievement in social studies in Telugu medium and English medium students.

So, the hypothesis that 'there is no significant association between Socio-Economic status and achievement in Social studies in Telugu medium and English medium Secondary School student's can be accepted.

Hypothesis 4 E : There is no significant association between Socio-Economic Status and achievement in Social studies in Boys and Girls.

Chi-square were computed to test the validity of the above hypothesis.

Table 4.42 : Association between SES and Achievement in Boys and Girls

Variable	Sample size	Chi-square
Boys	350	13.23*
Girls	350	3.13+

* Significant at 0.01 level.
\+ Not significant at 0.01 level.

As per the chi-square values, there was a significant relationship between socio-economic status and achievement in Social Studies in boys and it was not there in girls.

Consequently, the hypothesis that 'there is no significant association between socio-economic status and achievement in social studies in boys and girls' can be partially accepted and partially rejected.

Relationship between educational Aspirations and Achievement in Social Studies

As the present study aims at the identification of the relationship between educational aspirations and achievement in Social Studies, the following statistical treatment was given to the data.

Hypothesis 5 : There is no significant association between educational aspirations and achievement in Social Studies in Secondary School students.

To test the validity of the hypothesis, the chi-square values were calculated.

Table 4.43 : Association between Educational Aspirations and Achievement in Social Studies.

Sample	Sample size	Chi-square
Whole	700	20.13 *

* Significant at 0.01 level.

There was a positive significant relationship between educational aspirations and achievement in Social Studies in the Secondary School students.

So, the hypothesis that 'there is no significant association between educational aspirations and achievement in Social Studies in Secondary School students' can be rejected.

*Hypothesis 5 A : **There is no significant association between educational aspirations and achievement in social studies in residential and non-residential secondary school students.***

Chi-square values were calculated to test the validity of the above hypothesis.

Table 4.44: Association between Educational Aspirations and Achievement in Residential and Non-Residential Students

Variable	Sample size	Chi-square
Residential	350	4.23 +
Non-Residential	350	14.42 *

+ Not significant at 0.01 level.
* Significant at 0.01 level.

There was a significant association between educational aspirations and achievement in non-residential students and it was not there in residential students.

So, the hypothesis that 'there is no significant association between educational aspirations and achievement in Social Studies in residential and non - residential secondary school students' can be partially rejected and partially accepted.

Hypothesis 5 B : There is no significant association between Educational Aspirations and Achievement in Social Studies in Rural and Urban Secondary School students.

To test the validity of the above hypothesis, chi-square values were calculated.

Table 4.45 : Association between Educational Aspirations and Achievement in Rural and Urban Students

Variable	Sample size	Chi-square
Rural	350	7.99 +
Urban	350	18.41 *

+ Not significant at 0.01 level.
* Significant at 0.01 level.

There was a positive relationship between educational aspirations and achievement in urban students, and it was not present in rural students.

So, the hypothesis that 'there is no significant association between educational aspirations and achievement in Social Studies in rural and urban secondary school students' can be partially rejected and partially accepted.

Hypothesis 5 C : There is no significant association between educational aspirations and achievement in Social Studies in private and government secondary school students.

Chi-square values were computed to test the validity of the above hypothesis.

Table 4.46 : Association between Educational Aspirations and Achievement in Private and Government School Students

Variable	Sample size	Chi-square
Private	400	7.05 +
Government	300	14.77 *

+ Not significant at 0.01 level.
* Significant at 0.01 level.

The students of Government schools, unlike their counterparts of private schools, presented an association between their educational aspirations and achievements.

So, the hypothesis that 'there is no significant association between educational aspirations and achievement in Social studies in private and government school students' can be partially rejected and partially accepted.

Hypothesis 5 D : There is no significant association between educational aspirations and achievement in Social Studies in Telugu medium and English medium Secondary School students.

To test the validity of the above hypothesis, chi-square values were calculated.

Table 4.47 : Association between Educational Aspirations and Achievement in Telugu medium and English Medium Students

Variable	Sample size	Chi-square
Telugu medium	400	12.51*
English medium	300	5.64 +

* Significant at 0.01 level.
+ Not significant at 0.01 level.

There was a significant association between educational aspirations and achievement in Telugu medium students, and it was not present in English medium students.

So, the hypothesis that 'there is no significant association between educational aspirations and achievement in Social Studies in Telugu medium and English medium secondary school students' can be partially accepted and partially rejected.

Hypothesis 5 E : There is no significant association between educational aspirations and achievement in social studies in boys and girls.

Chi-square values were calculated to test the validity of the above hypothesis.

Table 4.48 : Association between Educational Aspirations and Achievement in Boys and Girls

Variable	Sample size	Chi-square
Boys	350	9.35 *
Girls	350	9.24 *

* Significant at 0.01 level.

There was a significant association between educational aspirations and achievement in both boys and girls.

So, the hypothesis that 'there is no significant association between educational aspirations and achievement in Social Studies in boys and girls' can be rejected.

5

SUMMARY, CONCLUSIONS AND DISCUSSION

SUMMARY OF THE STUDY

Education is human enterprise. It is a continuous effort to develop all capacities of the child, to control his environment and fulfil his requirements. It is an attempt on the part of the adult members of the society to shape the natural and gradual development of coming generations. It is directed towards desirable goals which are fixed by the society according to individual and social needs. Education is also an integrated growth, leading to enlargement of physical organs and maturity of mental capacities. Every child interacts with his environment, which tends to change towards the better.

Education is both a product and a process. As a process it involves the act of learning. As a product it is what we receive through learning, i.e., the knowledge, ideas and techniques. In a broader sense, all experiences and acts that have a formative effect on mind, character or physical activity of an individual are of education. Education is a process, by which society, through schools, colleges, institutions and universities deliberately transmits its cultural heritage, its accumulated knowledge, values and skills from one generation to the next.

One of the most important outcomes of any educational set-up is the achievement of the students. Depending on the level of achievement, individuals are characterized as high-achievers, average-achievers and low-achievers. The effectiveness of any educational system is gauged by the extent the students involved in the system achieve, whether it be in cognitive, conative or psychomotor domain. In general terms achievement refers to the scholastic or academic achievement of the student at the end of an educational programme. To maximize the achievement within a given set-up is the goal of every educationist. Many studies in different samples indicate, that the academic achievement is dependent on variables like set-up of educational institution, its organization, socio-economic status of students, their educational aspirations, and their well-adjusted behaviours.

Educationists are concerned with the plight of the socially disadvantaged. The social background such as home education, economic position, etc., of an individual decide his future efforts and achievements. The relationship between the socio-economic status and achievement of students will facilitate in drawing the suitable measures to enhance the student's prospects. The fruitful approach to study self-enhancement has been the concept of aspiration level. An individual's aspiration level represents him not only as he is at any particular moment, but also as who he would like to be best at some point in the future. It is a measure of his intentional disposition, an important element of his long range behaviour. So, it is necessary to have the knowledge of the educational aspiration level of student, both from educational and from guidance point of view.

Considering their role the variables selected for this study are: 1. residential versus non-residential secondary schools, 2. rural versus urban secondary schools, 3. private versus government secondary schools, 4. Telugu medium versus English medium secondary schools, and 5. boys versus girls.

The objectives of the present study were: 1. To find out the socio-economic status of secondary school students. 2. To find out the educational aspirations of secondary school students. 3. To find out the achievement in social studies of secondary school students. 4. To find out the relationship between socio-economic status and achievement in social studies. 5. To find out the relationship between educational aspirations and achievement in social studies of secondary school students. 6. To identify the difference in the level of socio-economic status, educational aspirations, achievement in social studies, relationship between socio-economic status and achievement in social studies, relationship between educational aspirations and achievement in social studies in secondary school students studying in residential and non-residential schools, private and government schools, rural and urban schools, Telugu medium and English medium schools, and in boys and girls.

Hypotheses were formulated taking into consideration the objectives. Hypotheses are formulated in Null form. The major hypotheses are : 1. The secondary school students do not possess high socio-economic status. 2. The secondary school students do not posses high educational aspirations. 3. The secondary school students do not possess high achievement in social studies. 4. There is no significant association between socio-economic status and achievement in social studies in secondary school students. 5. There is no significant association between educational aspirations and achievement in social studies in secondary school students. And sub-hypotheses were formulated according to the variable selected.

Stratified sampling technique, after making a detailed study of different techniques of sampling, was found to be the most appropriate technique for the present study. This technique was found to be the most suitable one because the present involves splitting of the sample into a good number of groups according to different variables. Through stratified sampling only it is possible to decide the sample into different groups or strata and choose students from each of these groups. Random sampling technique is also employed to select students from each group.

Regarding the size of the sample, 700 was found to be appropriate. This was found suitable because the study involves due intensity and detail, a sample with more than 700 students would involve a lot of resources, and the most important one, time. Fewer than 700 was students would also bring about problems of representativeness. Hence, 700 considered to be appropriate number for the sample, and this sample was selected from secondary schools. Out of this sample, the sub-group sample sizes are: residential 350, non-residential 350, rural 350, urban 350, private 400, government 300, Telugu medium 400, English medium 300, boys 350, girls 350.

Tools play a major role in any remake study as they are useful in the collection and analysis of data to draw conclusions and generalizations. As the study was a deliberate and intensive one, available standardized tools besides examination marks were used. The Socio-Economic Status Scale of Beena Shaw and Education Aspirations Scale of S.K. Saxena were selected. As these two scales were too lengthy and critical, the average marks of the whole year's exams were taken into consideration for assessing the achievement in Social Studies.

CONCLUSIONS AND DISCUSSION

Education plays a key role in building up of a beautiful society. A modern society cannot achieve its aims of economic growth, technical development, and cultural advancement without fully harnessing the talents of its citizens. Educationists thus strive to fully develop the intellectual potential of the students and make efforts to see that their potentialities are fully realized and channelized for the benefit of the individuals and that of the society.

Educational opportunities, though open to all, do not seem to engage to any reasonable extent the capacities of those who seek to utilize them. An eternal question baffling parents, educators and national planners is, why do students of demonstrated ability flop in their academic efforts at school or college examinations. Academic under-achievement more than academic failure, constitutes a grave problem as it amounts wastage of human resources which is construed as an irreparable loss to the society, which a developing country like ours can ill afford. So evaluation of achievement levels is necessary so as to plan the academic avenues.

At the time of appraisal of educational development, when many changes are being witnessed in organization, curricula and teaching techniques, it is pertinent to seek systematic and up-to-date information on the significant correlates of achievement. It was felt appropriate to identify the relationship of achievement in social studies with socio-economic status and educational aspirations along with their independent status in the secondary school students.

The present study has resulted in drawing the following conclusions.

SOCIO-ECONOMIC STATUS

1. The secondary school students were with middle socio-economic status

As the socio-economic status of the students plays a major role in academic excellence it is the duty of the parents to improve their socio-economic status by way of higher earnings, participation in community programmes, saving their earnings for future needs etc. The government and other social agencies are also supposed to help the low socio-economic status people to improve their status by way of implementing social welfare schemes. Once the socio-economic status of the parents is improved, they provide better educational facilities to their children. Even the confidence that gives the socio-economic status to a child will help him achieve well in all spheres of life. So every one in the society must try to direct the ladder of socio-economic status.

2. The students studying in residential and non-residential schools were with middle socio-economic status and there was no difference between them

Usually the private residential schools charge high fees for providing quality education. As the sample of residential schools was compared with that of students of government schools and private schools, the high socio-economic status of the students of private-residential schools might have been multiplied by the students of government residential schools. Whatever the reasons may be, as there was no significant difference in the socio-economic status of residential and non-residential school students, equal importance should be given to all in enhancing their socio-economic status. Scholarships and other educational facilities must be provided to the needy so as to get better education and to improve their socio-economic status further.

3. The rural and urban students were with middle socio-economic status and their was no significant difference between them

People in rural and urban areas are either well off or poor. The earnings and expenses of the urban community are considerably more than those of the members living in villages and small towns. The rural people are usually under-privileged, and can not afford much for the education of their children even after their high aspirations. It is upto every community member, government and voluntary agency to bring about improvement in the socio-economic status.

4. The students studying in private and government secondary schools were with middle socio-economic status and the private school students are with slightly higher socio-economic status

From the above information it seems clear that the students who study in private schools have better socio-economic status than their counter parts. The parents who have adequate economic resources and recognizable social status admit their children in private schools as they provide quality education and develop an all-round personality. Identifying the role of socio-economic status in getting better educational opportunities, it is necessary to develop each one's socio-economic status through various personal and social welfare programmes.

5. The Telugu medium and English medium students were with middle socio-economic status and the English medium students are with a recongnizable additional socio-economic status to their counter parts

Usually the schools which offer English as a medium [an international language] are managed by private trusts, societies and individuals. These schools charge high fees and the parents who can afford them only join their children in these English medium schools. The parents with good socio-economic status can afford English medium education and quality education in private schools. Every body in the society aspires for better education, but the socio-economic status restricts it. Hence, the socio-economic status is to be improved. And also the schools under government management and the schools which provide education through Telugu medium schools should also try to provide quality education and sound knowledge in English.

6. There was no significant difference in the level of socio-economic status of boys and girls, though both of them were with middle socio-economic status

As equal sample was taken from either sex and as they were taken from all types of schools, there was no significant difference in the level of socio-economic status of boys and girls. Educational facilities, scholarships, etc., may be provided equally to both boys and girls depending on their requirements.

EDUCATIONAL ASPIRATIONS

7. The secondary school students held an average level of educational aspirations

This results in acceptance with the study made in Guntur district by Hanumantha Rao (1998).

As the majority of the students decide their future courses at the end of the secondary level (as diversification of courses starts after the completion of this level), it is a dire necessity either to develop themselves by the students or to develop by the parents, teachers and society the educational aspirations to the optimum level. To develop educational aspirations to the potential level of the students, it is advisable to expose the students to various kinds of professions, different types of individuals who excelled in their careers, the people who work with great ambitions and the environments which show high quality and competence. Interests and ambitions may be enhanced, rewards and punishments may be used, and targets may also be fixed to develop high educational aspirations. And at the same time, educational aspirations must not be unrealistic as they put heavy pressure on tiny minds which leads to maladjustment.

8. The residential as well as non-residential students reveal significant educational aspirations, even though their performance is often average. The residential students possess educational aspirations higher than their counterparts

This result is in acceptance with the result of Hanumantha Rao [1998].

The students who join residential schools are from good socio-economic status and with higher intelligence than their counterparts. The educational atmosphere, the study schedule, the teaching learning process, the student activities are different from those of non-residential schools. The atmosphere, the competitive spirit, the intelligence, the teacher support might have contributed for this difference. The educational scenario that is prevailing in residential schools may be brought to the non-residential schools as far as possible. Also it is the duty of the responsible personnel and parents to develop high educational aspirations among the students to educate them and make them serve the society with great effect and efficiency.

9. The educational aspirations of rural and urban students were average and there was no difference between them

Normally it is believed that the urban students due to their exposure to many aspects, can possess higher educational aspirations than the rural students. This study, did not surprisingly find any such difference between in respect of the educational aspirations. Both of them can prove better in the area of education, provided equal opportunities were extended to them.

10. The educational aspirations of private and government school students were at an average level and there was no significant difference in the level of educational aspirations possessed by them

This result is against the result of Hanumantha Rao [1998] in which the government school students were with high educational aspirations than private school students.

Majority of people, for the purpose of education to their children, prefer private schools to the Government schools and pay the required fees as they ensure better education along with discipline. It is observed that regarding the educational aspirations, the students of both private and government schools give same response. It indicates that neither the facilities nor social background, stand in the way of their educational aspirations. Hence the concerned authorities should develop high educational aspirations among all the students.

11. The educational aspirations of English medium students were a little bit higher than the Telugu medium students though both of them were with an average level of educational aspirations

As the English medium schools are managed by private people, they provide better educational facilities to their children with full utilization of the resources available. The English medium students also get a better opportunity to go through various books available in English and because of this exposure they can develop higher educational aspirations. Under these situations, the authorities concerned are advised to make available good many books in Telugu by way of translation. Exposure to a wide variety of knowledge will definitely enhance the level of educational aspirations.

12. The educational aspirations possessed by boys and girls were at an average level and the boys are holding a little bit of higher educational aspirations than girls

This result is different from the result of Hanumantha Rao [1998].

The parents' ambitions, the boys' exposure to society, the expectations of the society might have contributed for the high educational aspirations of boys. If things are similar to both boys and girls, the educational aspirations of them will also be similar. So equal opportunities must be provided both for boys and girls to improve the status of educational aspirations.

ACHIEVEMENT IN SOCIAL STUDIES

13. The secondary school students were with high achievement in social studies

This result is in support of the studies of Bhaskara Rao [1989], Rathaiah [1993], Bhaskara Rao and Pushpalatha [1994], Rathaiah and Bhaskara Rao [1997]. The result of this study is contrary to the over-all achievement of the secondary school students in the state.

The factors contributing for this high achievement are many and multifarious. The competition among different types of schools, availability of adequate teaching learning facilities, conducive learning atmosphere, experience and efforts of teaching community, educational aspirations of students, socio-economic status of the demographical area, etc., might have contributed for this high achievement in social studies. If better educational facilities are provided, there will be no chronic under-achievement and the students will pass the examination in flying colours.

14. The achievement in social studies in residential and non-residential students was high and residential students were superior in achievement to their counterparts

Bhaskara Rao [1989], Rathaiah [1993], Bhaskara Rao and Pushpalatha [1994] and Rathaiah and Rao [1997] have found similar achievement in residential and non-residential students.

The facilities that are available in residential schools are no where available. The facilities such as libraries, laboratories, teaching learning strategies, learning atmosphere, study habits, institutional set-up, rapport between teacher and taught, expertise and commitment of teacher community, competitive spirit of students, intelligence and hard work of students might have helped for high achievement in social studies. The educational facilities and programmes that are available and in use should be extended to non-residential schools with in the perview of possibility.

15. The achievement in social studies in rural and urban students was high and the urban students were superior in achievement to their counterparts

This result stands contrary to the result of Bhaskara Rao (1989), Bhaskara Rao and Pushpalatha (1994) and in support of the studies of Pandey (1981) and Puric (1984).

The urban schools are usually with good infrastructural facilities when compared with rural schools. The students will also be engaged in educational activities unlike the rural students who spend their out-of-school time in agricultural pursuits. The urban parents are also well informed of the advantages of education than the illiterate and economically poor parents of rural areas. The rural students also show more interest in agricultural activities than educational programmes because of the economic constraints or of the problem of involing their minds in education rather than physique in agriculture. To be on par with urban students, the rural school children must be equipped with all educational facilities. The parents and students can be motivated in this regard.

16. The achievement in social studies was high in private and government school students and there was no significant difference in achievement in between these two groups

This result was in difference with the results of the studies of Rathaiah (1993), Rathaiah and Bhaskara Rao (1997) and in support of the results of the studies of Bhaskara Rao (1989) and Bhaskara Rao and Pushpalatha (1994).

Though the government schools are criticized for many reasons, the students studying in those schools secured high achievement in social studies. This may be due to their educational aspirations. Conducive educational atmosphere can be provided in both categories of the schools in order to boost the achievement levels.

17. The achievement in social studies was high in Telugu medium and English medium schools, and the English medium students possessed higher achievement than Telugu medium students

This result is in support of the studies of Bhaskara Rao (1989) and Bhaskara Rao and Pushpalatha (1994).

The English medium schools are located in urban areas and are run by private managements. These are well equipped in all aspects compared to Telugu medium schools. The students who pursue English medium educational also come from sound socio-economic status families. The awareness about the advantages of education will also be high in these students and their parents. The educational status and commitment of the English medium teachers will also be different from their counterparts. As these might have contributed for high achievement in English medium students, these must be extended to the Telugu medium students also.

18. The achievement in social studies was high in boys and girls and the boys performed a little better than girls

This result is in support of the studies conducted by Thakure (1972) and second International Science Study.

The slight difference in achievement that existed between boys and girls may be due to the availability of educational facilities and geographical differences. If equal opportunities are provided both boys and girls will achieve same results.

SOCIO-ECONOMIC STATUS AND ACHIEVEMENT IN SOCIAL STUDIES

19. There was no significant association between socio-economic status and achievement in social studies

This result supports the studies of Reddy, Nonzek, Salunke (1974), Chattarji, Mukherji and Banerjee (1971), Desai (1979), Rathaiah (1993), Rathaiah and Bhaskara Rao (1997) and opposes the results of Havighurst (1964), Menon (1973), Anand (1973), Abraham (1974), Basavaiah (1974), Lalithamma (1975), Das (1975),

Prakash Chandra (1975), Hemchandani (1980), Goswami (1978), Jain (1981), Shukla (1984), Mehrotra (1986), Misra (1986), Dwivedi (1983), Ramaswamy (1986), Sharma (1984), Sontakey (1986), Rajput (1984), Rathaiah and Bhaskara Rao (1997).

A positive influence of parents education on achievement has been observed in the studies of Clark [1927], Austin [1964], Basavayya [1974], Satyanandam [1969], Khanna [1980], Menon [1972], Ojha [1979], Chowdary [1975], Dave and Dave [1971], Grover [1979], Gaur [1982], Sankar [1983], Lall [1984], Jagannadhan [1985], Maitra [1985], Paul [1986], Trivedi [1987], Rathaiah and Rao [1997].

It is also found that there is a positive association between achievement and parent's occupation in the studies of Bear [1928], Austin [1964], Abraham [1974], Menan [1972], Ojha [1979], Dave and Dave [1971], Graven [1979], Gaur [1982], Sankar [1983], Lall [1984], Jagannadhan [1985], Maitra [1985], Paul [1986], Trivedi [1985], Rathaiah [1993], Mishra, Dash Padhi [1960], Grover [1979], Gaur [1982], Sankar [1983], Lall [1984], Maitra [1985], Paul [1985], Trivedi [1985].

Though this study did not show any association between achievement and socio-economic status of the students, many studies conducted earlier in this area have identified a positive relationship between these two.

The parents have to take due care of their socio-economic status as it has invariable influence on their children's achievement. They can improve their socio-economic status by educating and improving their educational qualifications, by that they can get promotions in their employment which improves their economic as well as social status. They can, even change their occupation depending on their educational qualifications and with the available financial resources. They can improve their home environment. From the government side also there is a great deal to be done to improve the economic status of the students as well as parents. The parents whose children are in educational institutions should be provided with adequate employment opportunities or work to earn their livelihood in order that their children can do better in studies without getting involved in child labour. Sufficient amount suitable to meet the educational as well as boarding and lodging requirements of the students through scholarships or at least as loans to the needy should be arranged. The students also should utilize properly the financial resources obtained either from parents or from government. If there is a student without any financial problem, he can excel in achievement.

20. The association between socio-economic status and achievement in social studies was significant in non-residential schools and insignificant in residential schools

This result may be because the students who pursue education in residential schools are with similar socio-economic status to some extent and the students of non-residential schools are from different walks of life. So the socio-economic status of all the needy must be improved through different modes and means.

21. There was no association between socio-economic status and achievement in social studies in both rural and urban students

As the sample is a mix of different types of schools and students, there might have been no relationship between achievement and socio-economic status. Still it is the duty of the concerned people to improve both socio-economic status and achievement.

22. There was no association between socio-economic status and achievement in social studies in both private and government school students

As there is no significant association between achievement and socio-economic status in government and private school students, one can say that the opinion that the rich people or socio-economically advantageous students study in private schools is not true. With this it seems that the students' choice in selecting a college depends on the teaching learning atmosphere of the institute. So the administrators of each and every college have to develop a conducive learning atmosphere in the classrooms irrespective of the availability of the infrastructural facilities.

23. There was no association between socio-economic status and achievement in social studies in both Telugu medium and English medium students

The language in which the students get education did not bring about any relationship between socio-economic status and achievement in social studies. The educational facilities may play a major role, so that they must be improved in all schools.

24. There was a positive association between socio-economic status and achievement in social studies among boys and it was not present among girls

Many people in our Indian society try to educate their male children rather than their female children. This may be due to the expectations kept on the male community or may be due to the customs and traditions of our society. So the males might be from high socio-economic status group when compared with the females. This study indicates that the girls with or without better socio-economic status are doing well in their education. So equal opportunities must be provided for both boys and girls.

EDUCATIONAL ASPIRATIONS AND ACHIEVEMENT IN SOCIAL STUDIES

25. There was a significant association between educational aspirations and achievement in social studies

The result of the present study supports the previous studies of Menon [1972], Gates [1948], Kuppuswamy [1974] and Hussain [1977]. At the same time it contradicts the studies of Gould and Kaplan [1940], Sears [1940], Holt [1942], Shultz and Ricciuti [1954], Sharma [1979], Muthayya [1962], Radha [1985], Rathaiah [1997] and Rathaiah and Bhaskara Rao [1997].

As the educational aspirations are very closely associated with the achievement in social studies, it is necessary to develop proper educational aspirations among all the students. If the educational aspirations of an individual are high, he will try to achieve those goals.

Aspirations are influenced by factors like-wishes for what individuals want to achieve; personal interests, which influence the areas of aspirations; the experiences with success strengthening aspirations and failures weakening them; the personality pattern, which influences both the kind and strength of aspirations; personal values, which determine what aspirations are more important; sex, with boys aspiring higher than girls; socio-economic status, with those of the middle and upper groups aspiring higher than those of lower groups; and racial background, with those of minority group status often aspiring unrealistically high in a form of compensation. Aspirations are also influenced by the environmental factors such as parental ambitions, which are higher in first-born than second-born children; social expectations, which emphasize that those who are successful in one area can be successful in all areas if they wish; peer pressures to set aspirations in areas important to the peer group; group emphasis on sex appropriateness of aspirations; cultural traditions which hold that all people can achieve anything they wish if they try hard enough; social values, which vary with the area of achievement; mass media, which encourages achievement aspirations; social rewards for high achievement and social neglect or rejection for low achievement; competition which siblings and peers have in the hope of showing one's superiority over them.

Whatever the conducive procedures may be, the parents and the teachers have to upgrade the positive educational aspirations among students, but this should not lead to frustration when the students fail to reach the level of aspiration. By promoting educational aspirations, one can improve the achievement of students as it has an influence on it.

26. There was no association between educational aspirations and achievement in social studies in residential students and it was present in non-residential students

Lack of association between educational aspirations and achievement in residential schools was due to the better socio-economic status and high educational aspirations of the residential students and the association that is present between educational aspirations and academic achievement may be due to the mix of various socio-economic status groups. Whether association between them is present or not, it is the duty of the parents and teachers to upgrade the educational aspirations for better achievement and for better professional selection.

27. There was no association between educational aspirations and achievement in social studies in rural students, but it was present in urban students

Educational aspirations usually promote the academic achievement. So the educational aspirations of both rural and urban students must be promoted to achievable levels so that they can settle well with their aspirations and abilities.

28. There was no association between educational aspirations and achievement in social studies in private school students but it was present in government school students

Though the government schools reflect less educational aspirations than their counterparts, their achievements are fairly remarkable. This situation is vice versa in case of private school students. So this result comes on to scene. The aspirations must be within limits and capable of achieving them, otherwise they will be of no use.

29. There was an association between educational aspirations and achievement in social studies in Telugu medium students and it was absent in english medium students

This result indicates that the educational aspirations of Telugu medium students are in accordance with their capabilities and the educational aspirations of the English medium students may be rising high without considering the realities. The educational aspirations may be promoted to the optimum level considering the students capabilities past and future.

30. There was association between educational aspirations and achievement in social studies in both boys and girls

As there is a significant positive association between educational aspirations and achievement in social studies, it is necessary to promote the educational aspirations of either sex to achieve equal and purposeful results.

SUGGESTIONS FOR FURTHER RESEARCH

The present study "*A study of Socio-Economic Status and Educational Aspirations of Secondary School Students in relation to their Achievement in Social Studies*" brings to light a good number of new areas to be studied by future researchers. The areas and variables which are not covered by this study may be put to test to enlighten the other associated factors of achievement. So, the researchers may think of the following areas to study in detail:

1. Studies on socio-economic status, educational aspirations and achievement may be extended to other levels of education, viz., primary, +2, graduation and post-graduation at district and state level.
2. Studies on the correlates of achievement in different subjects.
3. Studies may be taken in the above areas on experimental basis.
4. Studies may be conducted to identify the role of various psychological variable in enhancing the academic achievement.
5. Studies may be conducted to study the role of environmental factors by promoting educational aspirations and achievement.
6. Studies may be conducted to identify the the role of parents, teachers and society.

BIBLIOGRAPHY

Alpern, Morris L., "The Ability to Test Hypotheses". *Science Education* 30 (1946), 220-229.

Best, John W. *Research in Education,* 4th ed. New Delhi: Prentice Hall of India Pvt. Ltd., 1982.

Bhaskara Rao, D., e. d., Reforming School Education, New Delhi : Discovery Publishing House, 1998.

Bhaskara Rao, D. *Teacher Education in India.* New Delhi : Discovery Publishing House, 1998.

Bhaskara Rao, Digumarti. *A Comparative Study of Scientific Attitude, Scientific Aptitude and Achievement in Biology at Secondary School Level.* Unpublished Ph.D. Thesis, Osmania University, 1989.

Bhaskara Rao, Digumarti, ed. *Encyclopaedia of Education For all.* 5 Vols. New Delhi : APH Publishing Corporation, 1996.

Bhaskara Rao, Digumarti, ed. *International Encyclopaedic of Human Rights,* 10 vols. New Delhi : Discovery Publishing House, 2000.

Bhaskara Rao, Digumarti, ed. *International Encyclopaedia of AIDS,* 11 vols. New Delhi : Discovery Publishing House, 1999.

Bhaskara Rao, Digumarti, ed. *International Encyclopaedia of Science and Technology Education,* 11 vols. New Delhi: Discovery Publishing House, 2000.

Bhaskara Rao, D and D. Pushpa Latha. *Achievement in Science.* New Delhi : Discovery Publishing House, 1994.

Bhaskara Rao, Digumarti and Digumarti Pushpalatha, eds. *International Encyclopaedia of Women,* 5 vols. New Delhi: Discovery Publishing House, 1998.

Bhatia, K.K. *Measurement and Evaluation in Education.* Ludhiana: Prakash Brothers, 1991.

Biswas, A and J.c. Aggarwal. *Encyclopaedia Dictionary and Directory of Education, Vol. 1.* New Delhi : The Academic Publishers (India), 1987.

Biswas, A. and S.P. Agrawal. *Development of Education in India.* New Delhi: Concept Publishing Co., 1986.

Brandwein, Paul F., Fletcher G. Watson and Paul B. Blackwood. *A Book of Research Methods.* New York : Harcout, Brace World, Inc., 1958.

Bryan, I.F. and E.A. Locke. "Goal Setting as a Measure of Increasing Motivation', *Journal of Applied Psychology* 51 (1967), 274-277.

Buch, M.B., Chief Editor. *Fourth Survey of Research in Education.* New Delhi : NCERT.

Buch, M.B., Chief Editor. *Third Survey of Research in Education 1979-1983.* New Delhi: National Council of Educational Research and Training, 1984.

Buch, M.B., Editor. *Second Survey of Research in Education.* Baroda : Society for Educational Research and Development, 1979.

Chouhan, S.S. *Advanced Educational Psychology.* New Delhi : Vikas Publishing House Pvt. Ltd., 1978.

Coleman, James C. *Abnormal Psychology and Modern Life.* Bombay : D.B. Tarapolewala Co. (P) Ltd., 1969.

Desai, D.B. and Ameeta Govind. *Studies in Achievement Motivation.* Baroda : Centre for Advanced Study in Education, M.S. University of Baroda, 1979.

Ediger, Marlow and Digumarti Bhaskara Rao. *Science Curriculum.* New Delhi : Discovery Publishing House, 1997.

Ediger Marlow and Digumarti Bhaskara Rao. *Teaching Reading Successfully.* New Delhi: Discovery Publishing House, 2000.

Ediger, Marlow and Digumarti Bhaskara Rao. Teaching *Mathematics Successfully.* New Delhi : Discovery Publishing House, 2000.

English, H.B. and A.C. English. *A Comprehensive Dictionary of Psychoanalytical Terms.* London : Longmans, 1958.

Fergusan, George A. *Statistical Analysis in Psychology and Education.* 5th ed. Tokyo : Mc Graw-Hill International Book Co., 1981.

Festinger, Leon and Katz Daniel. *Research Mathods in the Bahavioural Sciences.* Amerind Publishing Co., 1976.

Festinger, L. "Theoretical Interpretation of Shifts in Level of Aspiration', *Psychological Review* 49 (1942), 235-250.

Freeman, Frank S. *Theory and Practice of Psychological Testing,* 3rd ed. Calcutta : Oxford and IBH Publishing Co., 1965.

Gage, N.L. *Handbook of Research on Teaching.* Chicago: Rand McNally & Co., 1966.

Garret, Henry E. *Statistics in Psychology and Education.* Bombay : Peffer and Simons Pvt. Ltd., 1979.

Gates, et.al. *Educational Psychology.* New York : The MacMillan Co., 1948.

Good, C.V., ed. *Dictionary of Education.* New York: MacGraw Hill Book Co., 1959.

Goode, William J. and Paul K. Hatt. *Methods in Social Research.* Tokyo : McGraw-Hill International Book Co., 1983.

Goode, William J. and Paul K. Hatt. *Methods in Social Research.* New York: McGraw-Hill Book Co., 1952.

Gravetter, Ferderick J. and Larry B. Wallnau. *Statistics for the Behavioural Sciences.* New Delhi: McGraw-Hill Publishing Co. Ltd., 1987.

Guilford, J.P. *Psychometric Methods.* New Delhi : Tata McGraw-Hill Publishing co. Ltd., 1987.

Harton, Paul B. and Chester L. Hunt. *Sociology.* Singapore : McGraw-Hill International Book Company, 1984.

Hurlock, Elizabeth B. Child Development, 6th ed. Auckland: McGrant-Hill International Book Company, 1978.

Jacobson, Willard J. and Rodney L. Doran. *Science Achievement in the United States and Sixteen Countries: A Report to Public* (Second IEA Science Study). New York : Teacher's College, Columbia University, 1988.

Jayswal, Sita Ram. *Techniques and Tests in Psychology and Education.* Lucknow : Prakasana Kendra, 1968.

Kaur, Gursharan. *Underachievement : Identification Diagnosis and Treatment.* New Delhi: Commonwealth Publishers, 1989.

Kerlinger, Fred N. *Foundations of Behavioural Research.* Holt, Rinehart & Winston, 1964.

Kundu, C.L. and D.N. Tutoo. *Educational Psychology.* New Delhi: Sterling Publishers Pvt. Ltd., 1985.

Hanumantha Rao, K. *A Study of the Educational Aspirations of Secondary School Students.* M.Ed. Dissertation, Nagarjuna University, 1998.

Kuppuswamy, B. *An Introduction to Social Psychology.* New Delhi: Asia Publishing House (P) Ltd., 1980.

Kuppuswamy, K. *A Textbook of Child Behaviour and Development.* Delhi: Vikas Publishing House, 1974.

Liebert, Robert M., Rita Wicks Poulos and Gloria Strauss Marmor. *Developmental Psychology,* 2nd ed. New Delhi: Prentice Hall of India Pvt. Ltd., 1979.

Lowel, E.K. and J.W. Atkinson. "The Effect of Need for Achievement on Learning and Speed of Performance', *Journal of Psychology* 33 (1953), 31-40.

Malla Reddy, M. *Student Unrest—A Socio-Psychological Study.* Department of Education, Osmania University, Hyderabad, 1988.

Mangal, S.K. *Educational Psychology.* Ludhiana : Prakash Brothers, 1991.

Marja, Talvi and Digumarti Bhaskara Rao, eds. Educational Leadership and Social Changes. New Delhi : Discovery Publishing House, 1996.

Morgan, clifford T., Richard A. King, John R. Weisz and John Schopler. *Introduction to Psychology,* 7th ed. New York : McGraw-Hill Book Co., 1986.

Muthayya, B.C. 'Level of Aspiration and Intelligence of High Achievers and Low Achievers in Scholastic Field', *Journal of Psychological Research* 9 (1962), 3.

Narayana Rao, S. *Educational Psychology*. New Delhi: Wiley Eastern Limited, 1990.

Parameswaran E.G. and C. Beena. *Invitation to Psychology*. New Delhi: Tata McGraw-Hill Publishing Co. Ltd., 1988.

Pearl, Richard E. 'The Present Status of Scientific Attitude Measurement : Hisotry, Theory and Availability of Measurement', *School Science and Mathematics* LXXIV (1974), 375-381.

Ramkumar, V. 'An Investigation into the Relationship of size of Family to Self-concept and Academic Achievement. *Edu. and Psych. Review.* XII (1972), 107-113.

Rastogi, K.G. *Educational Psychology.* Meerut: Rastgi Publications, 1983.

Rathaiah and D. Bhaskara Rao. *Achievement Correlates.* New Delhi: Discovery Publishing House, 1997.

Rathaiah, L. and Digumarti Bhaskara Rao, eds. *International Innovations in Education.* New Delhi : Discovery Publishing House, 1997.

Rummel, J. Francis. *An Introduction to Research Procedures in Education.* New York: Harper and Brothers, 1958.

Saxena, S.K. *Manual for Educational Aspiration Scale.* Agra : Agra Psychological Research Cell, 1989.

Sears, P.S. 'Level of Aspiration in Academically Successful and Unsuccessful Children', *Journal of Abnormal and Social Psychology* 35 (1940), 498-536.

Shah, Beena. *Manual for Socio-Economic Status.* Agra: Agra Psychological Research Cell, 1986.

Sharma, B.A.V., D.R. Prasad and P. Satyanarayana, editors. *Research Methods in Social Sciences.* New Delhi : Sterling Publishers Private Limited, 1989.

Sharma, Radha R. *Enhancing Academic Achievement—Role of Some Personality Factors.* New Delhi : Concept Publishing Co., 1985.

Smith, Edward W., Stanely W. Krouse and Mark M. Atkinson. *The Educator's Encyclopaedia.* New Jersey : Prentice Hall, 1969.

Taneja, V.R. *Educational Thought and Practice.* New Delhi : Sterling Publishers Pvt. Ltd., 1989.

Taylor, R.G. 'Personality Traits and Discrepant Achievement', *Journal of Counselling Psychology.* 11 (1964), 76-82.

Walberg, Herbert J. and Geneva D. Haertel, eds. *The International Encyclopedia of Educational Evaluation.* Oxford : Pergamon Press, 1990.

Veena Kumari, B. and D. Bhaskara Rao. *Operation Blackboard.* New Delhi : APH Publishing Corporation, 1996.

INDEX